BARBARIANS CHRISTIANS AND MUSLIMS

BARBARIANS CHRISTIANS AND MUSLIMS

Trevor Cairns

Published in cooperation with Cambridge University Press
Lerner Publications Company, Minneapolis

LIBRARY OF CONGRESS CATALOGING IN PUBLICATION DATA

Cairns, Trevor.
Barbarians, Christians, and Muslims.

(The Cambridge Introduction to History, v. 3)
SUMMARY: Traces the history of Europe from the dis-
integration of the Roman Empire through the rise of Islam,
with emphasis on the migrations of peoples and the spread
of Christianity.

1. Migrations of nations—Juvenile literature. [1. Europe—
History—392-814] I. Title.

D135.C3 1974   914′.03′11   73-20213
ISBN 0-8225-0803-6

This edition first published 1975 by Lerner Publications Company
by permission of Cambridge University Press.

Copyright © MCMLXXI by Cambridge University Press.
Original edition published as part of *The Cambridge Introduction to the History of Mankind.*

International Standard Book Number: 0-8225-0803-6
Library of Congress Catalog Card Number: 73-20213

Manufactured in the United States of America.

This edition is available exclusively from:
Lerner Publications Company, 241 First Avenue North, Minneapolis, Minnesota 55401

2 3 4 5 6 7 8 9 10 85 84 83 82 81 80 79

Contents

List of Maps and Diagrams p.vi
Editors' Note p.vii

Words and peoples p.4

The barbarians of the forests p.6

The barbarians move p.12

The barbarians of the plains p.14

The invasion of the West p.16
Attila, the 'scourge of God' p.18

The barbarians settle down: 'the Dark Ages' p.20

The end of Roman Britain: 'the Lost Centuries' p.22

The English come to Britain p.26

The long fight of the Britons p.30

Life in the English villages p.32
Land and water p.32
Fields p.32
Pasture and meadow p.36
The houses p.36
The hall p.38
The people p.38

The price of life p.39

The Christian church p.41
Bishops p.41
The Christian barbarians p.42
The Pope p.42
Hermits and monks p.42
Benedict and the Rule p.44

Christianity in Britain p.46
Christianity in Roman Britain p.46
Christianity reaches Ireland p.46
Irish monks and monasteries p.46

The conversion of the English p.50
The mission from Rome p.50
Roman monks in Northumbria p.52
Irish monks in Northumbria p.53
England is converted p.54
Roman or Irish p.55

The English scholars and saints p.58

Byzantium: the Rome of the East p.62

Muhammad: Prophet of Allah p.70

The conquests of the Arabs p.74

The civilization of Islam p.76

Charles the Great and his new Roman Empire p.80

The Northmen p.84

The defence of the West p.88

The kingdom of England p.90
The Great Army p.90
Alfred's fight p.90
The Viking settlements p.91
Alfred's defences p.91
One king of all England p.91
The Danes again p.94
1066 p.95

The Christian kingdoms of Europe p.96

Index p.97
Acknowledgments p.99

List of Maps and Diagrams

The three main European language groups of today; the boundary of the Roman Empire under Trajan, AD 98-117 *p. 5*

Other languages of Europe and the Mediterranean area *p. 5*

Territories of Germanic tribes before their invasion of the Roman Empire *p. 13*

Nomad hordes on the move *p. 15*

Goths enter the Eastern Roman Empire, 372-378 *p. 16*

Barbarians settling within the Roman Empire, about 450 *p. 17*

Attila the Hun in Western Europe, 451-2 *p. 19*

The Eastern Empire and the new barbarian kingdoms and settlements, about 600 *p. 20*

The invaders of Roman Britain *p. 22*

The late Roman military occupation of Britain: the last stage, 369 to about 410 *p. 23*

Jutish settlement in Kent *p. 26*

The conquest of mid-Britain *p. 27*

Kingdoms in Great Britain, about 600 *p. 29*

The Britons and the Anglo-Saxon advance, 600-800 *p. 31*

Excavation plan of part of an Anglo-Saxon settlement at Maxey, Northamptonshire *p. 37*

The patriarchates of Rome and Constantinople, about 600 *p. 43*

Irish influence in Britain and Europe to the end of the Seventh Century *p. 49*

Christianity leaps North, 625-32 *p. 52*

The struggle for Northumbria, 632-4 *p. 53*

The English converted from North and South *p. 55*

The kingdoms and bishoprics of England and Wales at the death of Bede, 735 *p. 56*

English influence in Europe during the Eighth Century *p. 61*

Defences of the Byzantine Empire in the later sixth century *p. 66*

Arabia about 570 *p. 71*

The conquests of Islam, 622-945 *p. 75*

The Frankish Empire and neighbouring peoples at the accession of Charles the Great, 768 *p. 81*

The empire of Charles the Great, 768-814 *p. 81*

The treaty of Verdun, 843 *p. 83*

The homelands of the Vikings *p. 84*

Vikings on the move *p. 87*

Christendom attacked by Vikings, Muslims and Magyars *p. 88*

Conquests of the Great Army and overthrow of the English kingdoms, 865-874 *p. 90*

England as divided between Alfred and the Danes; the Norse settlements in Britain, ninth to the eleventh centuries *p. 91*

The Kingdom of England *p. 92*

The empire of King Canute at his death, 1035 *p. 94*

The campaigns of 1066: the triumph of Duke William the Norman *p. 95*

Political and religious divisions of Europe in 1097 *p. 96*

Editors' Note

In preparing this edition of *The Cambridge Introduction to History* for publication, the editors have made only a few minor changes in the original material. In some isolated cases, British spelling and usage were altered in order to avoid possible confusion for our readers. Whenever necessary, information was added to clarify references to people, places, and events in British history. An index and a list of maps and diagrams were also provided in each volume.

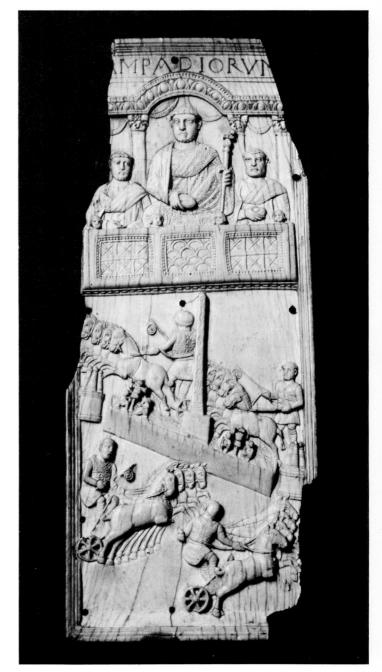

Words and peoples

ENGLISH	Hand	Valley	Green	Fish
BULGARIAN	Rŭká	Doliná	Zelén	Ríba
CZECH	Ruka	Údolí	Zelený	Ryba
DANISH	Hånd	Dal	Grøn	Fisk
DUTCH	Hand	Dal	Groen	Vis
FRENCH	Main	Vallée	Vert	Poisson
GERMAN	Hand	Tal	Grün	Fisch
ITALIAN	Mano	Valle	Verde	Pesce
NORWEGIAN	Hand	Dal	Grøn	Fisk
POLISH	Ręka	Dolina	Zielony	Ryba
PORTUGUESE	Mão	Valle	Verde	Peixe
RUMANIAN	Mân	Valeă	Verde	Peşte
RUSSIAN	Ruká	Dolína	Zelëny	Rýba
SERBO-CROAT	Ruka	Dolina	Zelen	Riba
SPANISH	Mano	Valle	Verde	Pescado
SWEDISH	Hand	Dal	Grön	Fisk
LATIN	Manus	Vallis	Viridis	Piscis

If you are reading this book, you are reading English.

If you lived in any other country of Europe, you would read and speak some other language.

In Europe there are almost as many different languages as there are countries, but although these languages are different, they are not *completely* different. Look at this list. It shows a few common words in the main European languages. If you examine the list carefully, you will be able to see which words seem very much the same in different languages, and so you will be able to put the languages into three groups or families.

We can make a map showing these groups of languages and the countries where they are spoken. Here it is, at the top of page 5. The three groups of languages are called:

LATIN (or ROMANCE). You will notice that these languages are spoken where the Romans once ruled in western Europe.

TEUTONIC (or GERMANIC). These are spoken in the lands which lay north and east of the old Roman frontier, the lands which the legions faced but never conquered.

SLAVONIC. These are spoken in eastern Europe, by peoples living beyond the Germanic lands.

These three great families of languages date back to the time of the Romans, and before, though the frontiers of the countries where they are spoken have changed very much since the Roman Empire broke down.

(Even these families, by the way, seem to be related, though very distantly. One or two words are much the same in all of them. The word for 'mother', for instance, is 'mater' in Latin, 'madre' in Spanish, 'mutter' in German, 'mat' in Russian.)

There are some languages which we did not put on the first map, because they do not belong to the three big families. Two of these languages date from before the Roman Empire. The CELTIC language of the Ancient Britons is still spoken by some people in Ireland, Wales, the Scottish Highlands and Brittany. The GREEK language, at the other end of the Roman Empire, was also too strong to be killed by Latin.

The other languages came to Europe later. They belong to invaders, nomads from the great plains of Asia whose children and grand-children settled down further west.

Finally, if we look to the south and east of the Mediterranean Sea, we shall see another great 'new' language, different from all the others: ARABIC.

One of the most important things in this book is the story of how the peoples who speak these languages settled down in the lands where they live today.

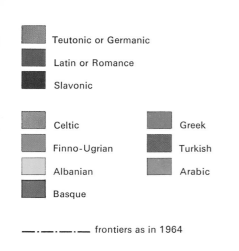

Teutonic or Germanic

Latin or Romance

Slavonic

Celtic

Finno-Ugrian

Albanian

Basque

Greek

Turkish

Arabic

—·—·—·— frontiers as in 1964

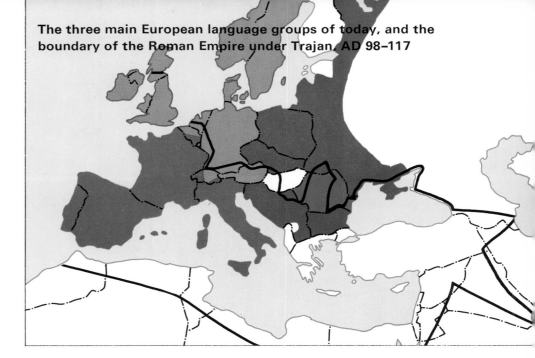

The three main European language groups of today, and the boundary of the Roman Empire under Trajan, AD 98–117

1 SCOTLAND	23 ITALY
2 N. IRELAND	24 YUGOSLAVIA
3 EIRE	25 ALBANIA
4 WALES	26 BULGARIA
5 ENGLAND	27 GREECE
6 NORWAY	28 TURKEY
7 SWEDEN	29 MOROCCO
8 FINLAND	30 ALGERIA
9 DENMARK	31 TUNISIA
10 THE NETHERLANDS	32 LIBYA
11 BELGIUM	33 EGYPT (U.A.R.)
12 LUXEMBURG	34 ISRAEL (Hebrew)
13 FRANCE	35 JORDAN
14 SPAIN	36 SAUDI ARABIA
15 PORTUGAL	37 THE LEBANON
16 GERMANY	38 CYPRUS
17 POLAND	39 SYRIA
18 CZECHOSLOVAKIA	40 IRAQ
19 SWITZERLAND	41 PERSIA
20 AUSTRIA	42 U.S.S.R.
21 HUNGARY	
22 RUMANIA	

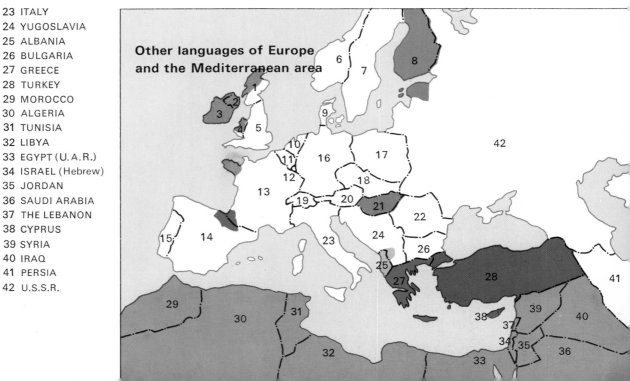

Other languages of Europe and the Mediterranean area

The barbarians of the forests

Village

The nations who came to live in the lands which had once been ruled by the Caesars were very unlike the former citizens of the Roman Empire. They believed in different gods, they had different customs, they lived in an altogether different way. The Romans called them barbarians. Of all these peoples, we know most about the Germanic tribes who lived just across the Rhine and Danube, where the Roman frontier was.

In the great forests these tribesmen lived a life that was not civilized. Their life was hard and rough, but it was free. They built their houses of logs, grew their crops in the more open parts of the country or where they had cleared the trees, they hunted and they fished. Roman pictures show us what they and their villages looked like. Their clothes and even their bodies have also been found sometimes in the bogs of Denmark and north Germany, strangely preserved by chemicals in the damp soil. Here also there have been found many weapons, which had been ceremonially buried or 'sacrificed'. These tribesmen were brave and warlike, often fighting among themselves or against the Romans. Often, too, they enlisted in the Roman army, and faithfully fought for the emperor.

In their own lands, the tribesmen were not ruled by an emperor. They had no governors and tax-collectors, no judges and lawyers – not even written laws. When anything important had to be decided, the men would hold a meeting (or 'moot', or 'thing', as it was sometimes called in different places). They would advise their king or chief, or elect a new one. They might have to decide on peace or war, consider the state of the harvest, try a thief or a murderer. These tribesmen were so free that some Romans said that the Germans had the sort of freedom which the Caesars had taken from the Roman people.

Council

Electing the chief

The Damendorf Man. The chemicals in the peaty soil of Schleswig, where he lay buried for about 1,500 years until his discovery in 1900, preserved his flesh, skin and hair, but not his bones. His garments had been placed over his corpse; the shoes and belt can be seen in the photograph.

below: Swords found at Kragehul, Denmark. They and other weapons had apparently been sunk in a bog as a sacrifice. Hilts and scabbard mounts of silver (*top*) and bronze (*below*) remained on the rusted weapons. At the bottom is a well-preserved blade with its wooden scabbard.

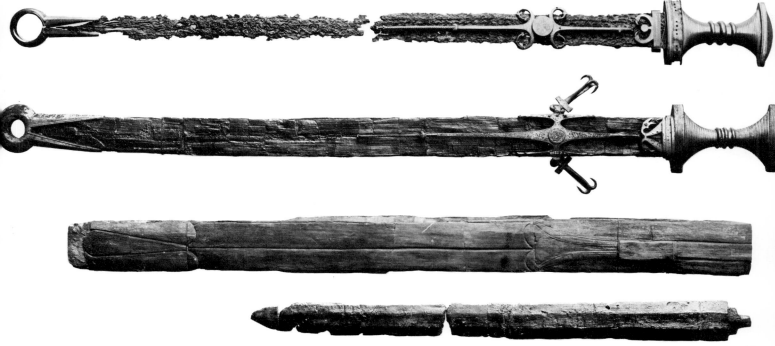

THE SUTTON HOO
TREASURE

below: Jewelled gold buckle,
3 in. (76 mm) long.

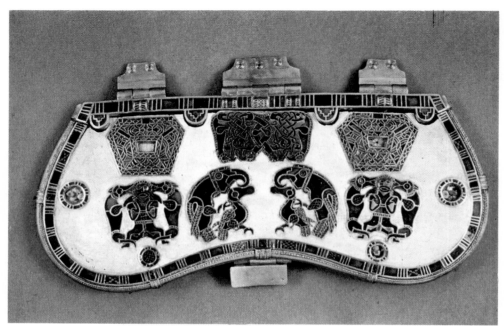

top left: Purse-lid, 7·35 in. (187 mm) wide; 4·1 in. (101 mm) high.

below left: Hinged gold clasp decorated with garnets. Opened width is 4·45 in. (113 mm); height is 2·05 in. (52 mm).

In 1939, at Sutton Hoo in Suffolk, a ship was discovered, buried in a great mound. Though the timbers had rotted away, their pattern and rows of corroded rivets remained pressed into the sandy soil. The ship had been an open war-boat 89 ft (27 m) long, and within it were rich treasures such as may have belonged to a king. No corpse lay with them. Perhaps the burial was in memory of a seventh-century king of East Anglia who had disappeared in a lost battle.

above: Jewelled gold ornaments from the sword knot, 0·55 in. (14 mm) wide at the base.

left: The great gold buckle, 5·2 in. (132 mm) long.

There is a big difference, though, between being free and running wild. These tribesmen had their laws, even though they were not written down. They knew what was right and what was wrong, and what the customs of their people were. Every man was supposed to be truthful, loyal and brave, and to do his duty.

First, a man had to be loyal to his family, or kin. If one of the kin were robbed or hurt or killed, all the other men in the family would demand repayment from the man who had done the damage. Sometimes they might refuse to accept compensation, and decide to kill the man who had injured them. If that happened a blood feud between two families could easily start. Often, however, matters could be put right at the moot. So a man helped his kin, and his kin helped him.

There was another loyalty which could be even more important than loyalty to the kin. This was loyalty to a man's lord. In a village there would sometimes be a large wooden hall. Here the chief or the king lived with his slaves, his servants, his family – and his chosen warriors. These were men who had come to the chief and asked if they could become members of his band of 'Companions'. Once the chief accepted them, he became their 'Lord'. They lived in his hall and ate at his table. In the evenings, by the light of the huge fire burning on the open hearth in the midst of the hall, they would feast on their lord's meat, drink his ale and mead from the horns, and listen to minstrels singing of the great deeds of heroes of the past; or, sometimes, of their lord and themselves, if they had won a fight. (In some ways this was very like the life of the warrior-kings about whom Homer had made epic poems over a thousand years before, but now the scene was not the sunlit Aegean Sea but the sombre northern forests.) The lord would bestow gifts upon his warriors – rings and bracelets of gold, fine helmets and mail-shirts, richly adorned swords with blades cunningly pattern-welded for beauty and for strength.

Evening in the chieftain's hall. The tables have been cleared away, and the warriors exult in songs of heroic fighting.

Ringkobing Firth on the west coast of Denmark. This is the sort of shore that the Anglo-Saxons left when they sailed for Britain, the bleak mixture of land and sea that the Wanderer knew too well.

It was a fine life for a warrior, to enjoy the protection and friendship of a good lord. There is a poem of one of these barbarian nations, the Anglo-Saxons, which tells of the feelings of a warrior who has lost his lord: 'the friendless man wakes again, sees before him the dark waves, the sea-birds bathing, spreading their feathers; frost and snow falling mingled with hail'. And the Wanderer – that is the title of the poem – thinks of the good times he once enjoyed, feasting with the warriors in the firelit hall.

In return for all this, a 'companion' owed to his lord complete loyalty, especially in battle. These chosen men must make sure that, even in the fiercest fight, their lord was safe. If he were killed, they must avenge his death by killing the enemy. If the enemy were too strong, they must die fighting over the body of their lord. It was very simple.

These lords and warriors lived in order to win fame and treasure. If they were lucky, songs would be sung about their famous fights long after they were dead. Anyway, if a man wanted wealth he had to fight to get it. An ordinary villager could live on the crops and the herds of swine and cattle; he had plenty of wood and leather; his wife could spin wool; local smiths and carpenters could fashion the tools, utensils, carts, weapons that he needed. But it was different for a lord. He had to give his warriors gifts which did not grow in forest or field, which were beyond the skill of a village craftsman to make. The coloured pictures on pages 8 and 9 show you the treasure belonging to a great lord – perhaps a king – of the Anglo-Saxons who settled in Britain. Look at the richness and beauty of the gold and jewels and enamel. Then think of the life of an ordinary villager, an ordinary working peasant. His life was one of hard work, and there was always danger of death by injury, or illness, or sheer starvation if the crops failed. This may help you to understand even better how many of these people thought that the finest life for a man was to fight and feast in the war-band of a powerful and generous chief.

The barbarians move

There was nothing new in tribes and nations wandering. You may remember how wave after wave of prehistoric people had come to Britain, or how the Gauls had invaded Italy, or how Marius and Sulla and Julius Caesar had all in turn fought against armies of wandering Germans. We do not know for certain why they wandered, but it is likely that often they were looking for more fertile lands or a better climate.

Remember, too, that it was fairly easy for these people to move. Their houses were simply made of wood, clay and thatch. They could soon build new ones if they did not capture suitable houses in the lands to which they came. Their other belongings could quickly be piled into a cart or slung across the back of a horse. Barbarian tribes could migrate in a way that would not be possible for more civilized people, used to better houses with more in them.

Probably the Germanic tribes had never really been still. If you look at the next map you will see where their most important tribes lived just before they moved into the Roman Empire, about the year 375. You will notice that the Goths, especially the Ostrogoths, had come a long way from the island of Gotland. They must have collected a lot of recruits

Barbarians moving

on their way, because they had become a big and strong people.

These tribes seem to have been pushing and jostling each other. Some, like the Franks, were up against the Roman frontier. Others, like the Frisians and the Saxons, were on the marshy coast of the North Sea. At the opposite end the Ostrogoths were on the steppe-lands by the Black Sea. It is easy to see how the Frisians and Saxons became good seamen, while the Goths, learning from the nomads they met on the steppes, became good horsemen.

These barbarians might have gone on wandering and shoving one another without doing much harm to the Roman Empire. But they themselves were now attacked by a new horde of terribly ferocious barbarians who came sweeping out of the endless plains of Asia – the Huns.

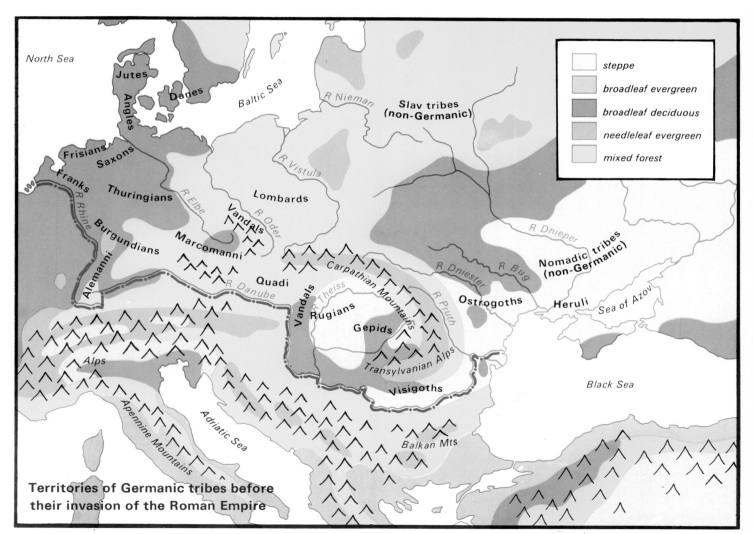

Territories of Germanic tribes before their invasion of the Roman Empire

The barbarians of the plains

Horse-archer in action. The Romans knew this style of shooting as a Parthian shot. There are no good pictures of nomad warriors of the fifth century, and this Turkish painting was made a thousand years later; but the weapons and tactics almost certainly remained much the same.

Where the forests ended, the steppes began. These enormous plains, sometimes fairly fertile and sometimes no better than deserts, stretched from beside the Black Sea all the way across Asia. Only in a few places, where cities like Samarkand and Bokhara were built, was the land good enough for growing crops. On the plains the only people who could live were the nomadic tribes.

These people were Mongolian. They were small, stocky men with flattish faces, high cheekbones and yellowish skin. Their legs were often bent, because they spent all their time on horseback. They had no homes, but went with their herds —

especially herds of horses – wherever there was pasture. Their families camped with them, in tents. Their food was meat, often eaten half-raw; and their drink was milk, sometimes fermented. They had no possessions except what they could carry with them.

They lived a hard life in a hard land; only hard people could survive. They despised people who lived in cities or on farms, and thought that such people were fit only to be robbed, enslaved and killed. When it came to killing, these nomads were experts. They used a short bow, made of horn and sinew, very powerful but convenient for shooting from the back of a horse. They could ride round their enemies, shooting them down. If the enemy tried to charge them, the nomads would scatter – and then return to the attack as soon as the enemy was tired. So these nomads could overwhelm most armies, while they would never allow themselves to be hit by a heavier and stronger enemy.

Such tribes were always a menace to more civilized or settled peoples who lived near the edges of the great steppes. Sometimes the menace became deadly, when there arose some outstandingly clever chief among the nomads. A man like that would sometimes be able to bring together a large number of tribes, and so make up a huge army of mounted bowmen. When this happened, the nomads could topple kingdoms and empires.

From time to time, all through history, the civilizations near the steppes have been forced to fight for their lives against the nomads, and sometimes they have been conquered. As you know, the Chinese had built the Great Wall before 200 B.C., but even this did not always hold back the hordes. India and Persia were not always safe behind their mountain barriers. In the west, the Slavonic and Germanic tribes lay between the nomads and the Roman Empire. Now the Huns, fiercest of all the nomads, were on the move. Some pushed south, against India. Others moved west.

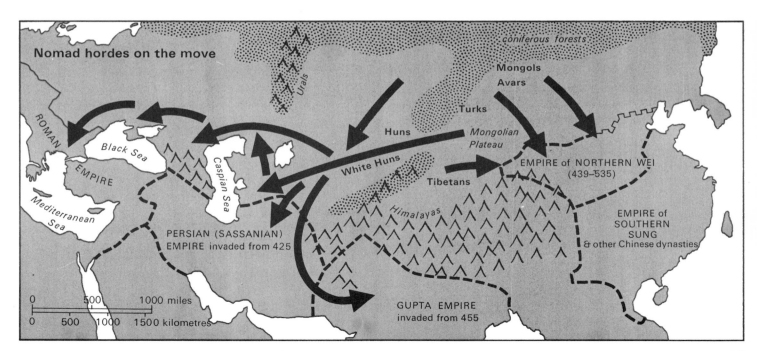

The invasion of the West

In the year 372 the Goths collided with the Huns. The Goths were so badly beaten that they staggered back towards the river Danube. Across the Danube was the Roman Empire. The Goths asked to be allowed to come in and settle down. In return, they promised to hold the frontier for the Romans.

The emperor, who was living in Constantinople, agreed. This sort of thing had happened before, on several frontiers. It had usually worked well, especially as the population inside the Roman Empire seems to have been getting smaller, so that there was room for settlers from outside. The Goths were the largest group of people who had ever come in, but there was no reason to think that they would behave badly.

At first all went well. Then the emperor's tax-collectors caused trouble, and fighting began. There was a great battle in 378 at Adrianople, and the big mail-clad Goth horsemen caught the Roman army at a disadvantage and wiped it out. The emperor himself was among the slain.

From now on, though new Roman armies were raised and new emperors appointed, things became very confused and complicated. Different tribes and nations of Germanic barbarians moved into the Empire. Sometimes they came because the emperor paid them to fight for him; sometimes they broke in to loot. There was an eastern Roman emperor in Constantinople, and a western emperor who usually lived now in Milan or Ravenna. There were tribes of Franks, Saxons, Vandals, Goths. It was very hard to tell who was helping whom against whom.

This will give you an idea of what it was like.

The Goths, under King Alaric, marched in 401 from the Eastern Empire into the Western Empire. They were met by the western Roman army. Most of the 'Roman' soldiers were barbarians themselves, and the 'Roman' general was a Vandal called Stilicho, whose daughter was the wife of the western emperor. Stilicho beat Alaric, but the emperor now became afraid that he was too powerful, so in 408 he had him murdered. This gave Alaric his chance, especially as some of Stilicho's men refused to fight any longer for the emperor. Alaric and his Goths invaded Italy. The emperor made a treaty with them, and broke it. As revenge, in 410 Alaric took Rome and looted the city; though he took care not to damage it badly, because he felt admiration and respect for the wonderful mother-city of the Empire. Soon afterwards Alaric died. While all this was happening, Vandals and Sueves had broken into Gaul and Spain. Now the western emperor offered to give part of Gaul to the Goths if they would go there and drive out the Vandals. So the Goths left Italy in 412, beat the Vandals and settled in Gaul in 417. The Vandals moved on to Spain and Africa.

You may think that all this is very confusing. It is – and you have heard only one or two of the most important things. Fortunately, there is no need to remember all the details. You may, though, have noticed one or two things that are worth remembering. The next map, which shows the position in 450 approximately, should help you.

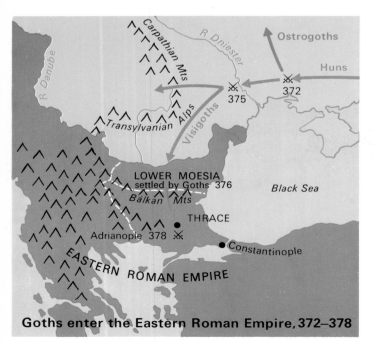

Goths enter the Eastern Roman Empire, 372–378

First, the Eastern Empire was practically unharmed, for the barbarian nations had drifted westwards. This was partly because in the Eastern Empire there were better emperors, much more money, and a far better army and navy.

Second, even in the Western Empire the barbarians were not trying to destroy it. They were trying to settle down and to become the masters of parts of the Empire, which is very different from destroying. Some of the barbarian chiefs, like Alaric, were intelligent men who valued the achievements of the Roman Empire. They wanted to share in the benefits of Roman civilization.

Of course, there was bound to be a lot of destruction, because of all the fighting. There was a lot of looting, robbery and murder. Then, when they had settled, the barbarians were often too ignorant or careless to be able to run things as the Roman governors and civil servants had done. Buildings began to fall into decay, water supplies to fail, roads to wear out, and often there were too few engineers and architects to maintain or replace them properly. Educated men, lawyers and teachers and doctors, for example, became fewer in the lands ruled by barbarians. This may have been because there were too few good jobs for them where the power was in the hands of warrior-chiefs and their chosen 'companions', and because their ideas did not fit in well with the manners and customs of the barbarians.

Life under the barbarians may have been more rough and ready than before they came; but it is wrong to think, as many people do, that these barbarians were no more than a mob of wilfully destructive hooligans. It is just as wrong to think of the barbarian invasions as a simple story of civilized Romans on one side being overwhelmed by hordes of savages on the other. The truth, as usual, was more complicated and less dramatic.

But there were some terrible attackers who had no wish to settle, men who thoroughly earned their terrible name as cruel savages.

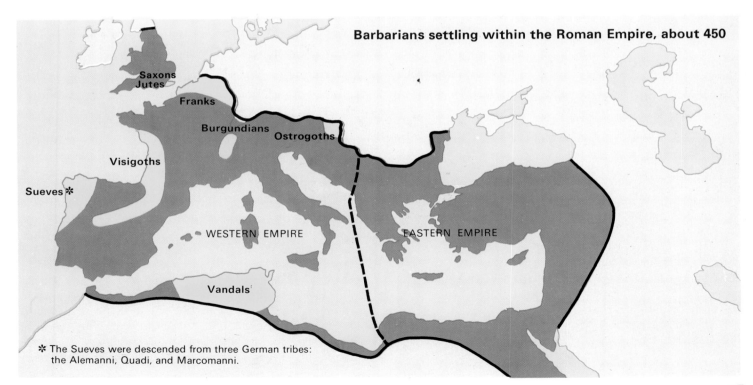

Barbarians settling within the Roman Empire, about 450

Saxons
Jutes
Franks
Burgundians
Ostrogoths
Visigoths
Sueves ✶
WESTERN EMPIRE
EASTERN EMPIRE
Vandals

✶ The Sueves were descended from three German tribes: the Alemanni, Quadi, and Marcomanni.

Attila, 'the scourge of God'

The Huns came smashing into an Empire that was already splitting. Their leader was Attila. Wherever he went, he conquered. He forced all the tribes who lived east of the Rhine, Germans and Slavs, to obey him and to join his army; but the Huns themselves remained his most deadly warriors. To the Romans, who were now all Christians, the Huns seemed to be devils. Their faces, ugly and savage naturally, were made worse by the scars which ran down their cheeks. These, so it was said, were caused by hot irons which the Huns thrust against the faces of baby boys; some said to prevent their beards from growing, some said to teach them to bear pain. As for Attila himself, Christians thought he must have been sent by God to punish mankind for its wickedness, and they called him 'the scourge of God'. Wherever they went, the Huns brought terror, destruction and death.

Even 'the scourge of God', however, could be stopped. In 451 Attila led his hordes into Gaul. Here the general of the Roman army joined forces with the chiefs of the tribes that had settled down. Romans, Goths, Franks and Burgundians together formed a mighty host. Near the town which is now called Châlons, Attila crashed into it – and stopped. Neither side was really beaten, but this was the first time that anyone had stood up to Attila and survived. Attila swerved away with the loot he had already won.

In 452 he struck south, into Italy. He killed and burned as no other barbarian had. His hordes flowed towards Rome itself. Then Attila was stopped again. This time it was not a great army which stood in his path, but one man, the Christian bishop of Rome, Pope Leo. He came out from the city and asked Attila, the man who knew no mercy, to spare Rome. And Attila did as the Pope asked. Why he did it we do not know. There was famine and disease in Italy, and Attila may have wished to get away quickly, before his army suffered. A powerful force was known to be marching from the Eastern Roman Empire, to try to cut him off. He, or some of the Christians in his horde (for many of the barbarians were learning Christianity), may have feared that the Pope had supernatural powers. Whatever the reason, the fact is that he turned back once more with his plunder, and went back to his camp on the Hungarian plain.

left: The Huns —
as they appeared to the people they
attacked.

1. Natural shape of bow

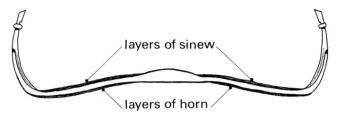

layers of sinew

layers of horn

A composite bow. The powerful spring comes not
from the wooden centre, but from the pull and push
of the sinew and horn. Though size and shape may have
varied slightly, Hun bows must have been of this type.

2. Bow strung
ready for use

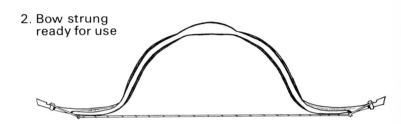

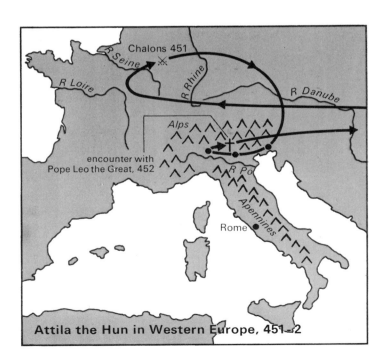

Attila the Hun in Western Europe, 451–2

In 453 he planned another great raid, this time into the
Eastern Empire. Before he could begin he burst a blood-vessel
one night, and so he died.

With Attila dead, his horde broke up. That was always the
weakness of savage armies, which could only be held together
by tremendously strong leaders. Now the German tribes whom
Attila had conquered rose against the Huns and shattered
them, and drove the survivors eastwards. Within a few years, all
that remained of the enormous horde were a few nomad tribes,
wandering once more on the steppes from which they had come.
Attila, like many another great nomad leader, left behind him
nothing but a name for vast slaughter and destruction; one
who could destroy all things and make nothing.

19

The barbarians settle down: 'the Dark Ages'

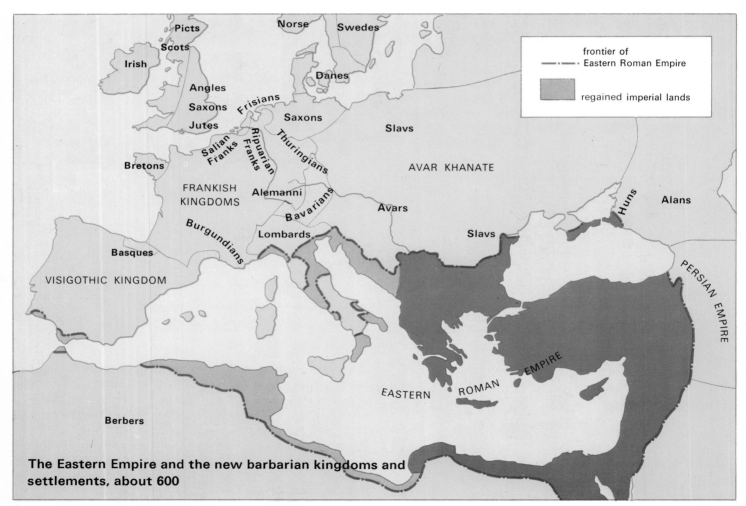

frontier of
Eastern Roman Empire

regained imperial lands

Picts

Norse   Swedes

Scots

Irish

Danes

Angles

Saxons   Frisians

Jutes   Saxons

Salian   Ripuarian   Thuringians

Franks   Franks

Bretons

FRANKISH
KINGDOMS   Alemanni

Burgundians   Bavarians

Lombards

Basques

VISIGOTHIC KINGDOM

Berbers

Slavs

AVAR KHANATE

Avars

Slavs   Huns   Alans

PERSIAN EMPIRE

EASTERN   ROMAN   EMPIRE

**The Eastern Empire and the new barbarian kingdoms and
settlements, about 600**

The disappearance of the Huns left the Germanic invaders of the Western Empire to settle as best they could. As they settled, it became more and more obvious that nobody was taking any notice of the emperor, until at last, in 476 a barbarian chief deposed the last western Roman emperor and made himself king in Italy. It was the end of the Roman Empire in the west. Something great had ended, and historians have often been so impressed by this that they have called the next few centuries 'the Dark Ages'. When you have learned as much as you can about the new kingdoms of the barbarians, you can decide whether or not you think everything was as dark as the name suggests.

In the Eastern Empire the emperors who ruled in Constantinople held back the barbarians from their provinces. Meanwhile, the Slavonic tribes were spreading south and west behind the Germanic tribes. The map shows you what was happening about the year 600.

For the time being, we shall not look at the barbarian peoples in the north and east of Europe, nor at the Eastern Roman Empire. The main thing to notice is that the Visigoths in Spain and the Franks in Gaul were managing to set up reasonably strong and steady kingdoms. The modern states of France (you can see how Gaul got its new name) and Spain were having their foundations laid. But if you look back to the first pages in this book you will see that in both of these countries the Latin language won. The Germanic warriors may have been strong enough to become the masters, but they were too few to change the language of the people they had conquered.

In England things turned out differently. Here a Germanic language overcame both the Latin and the Celtic languages. It is time for us to look more closely at what happened when the barbarian invaders reached Britain.

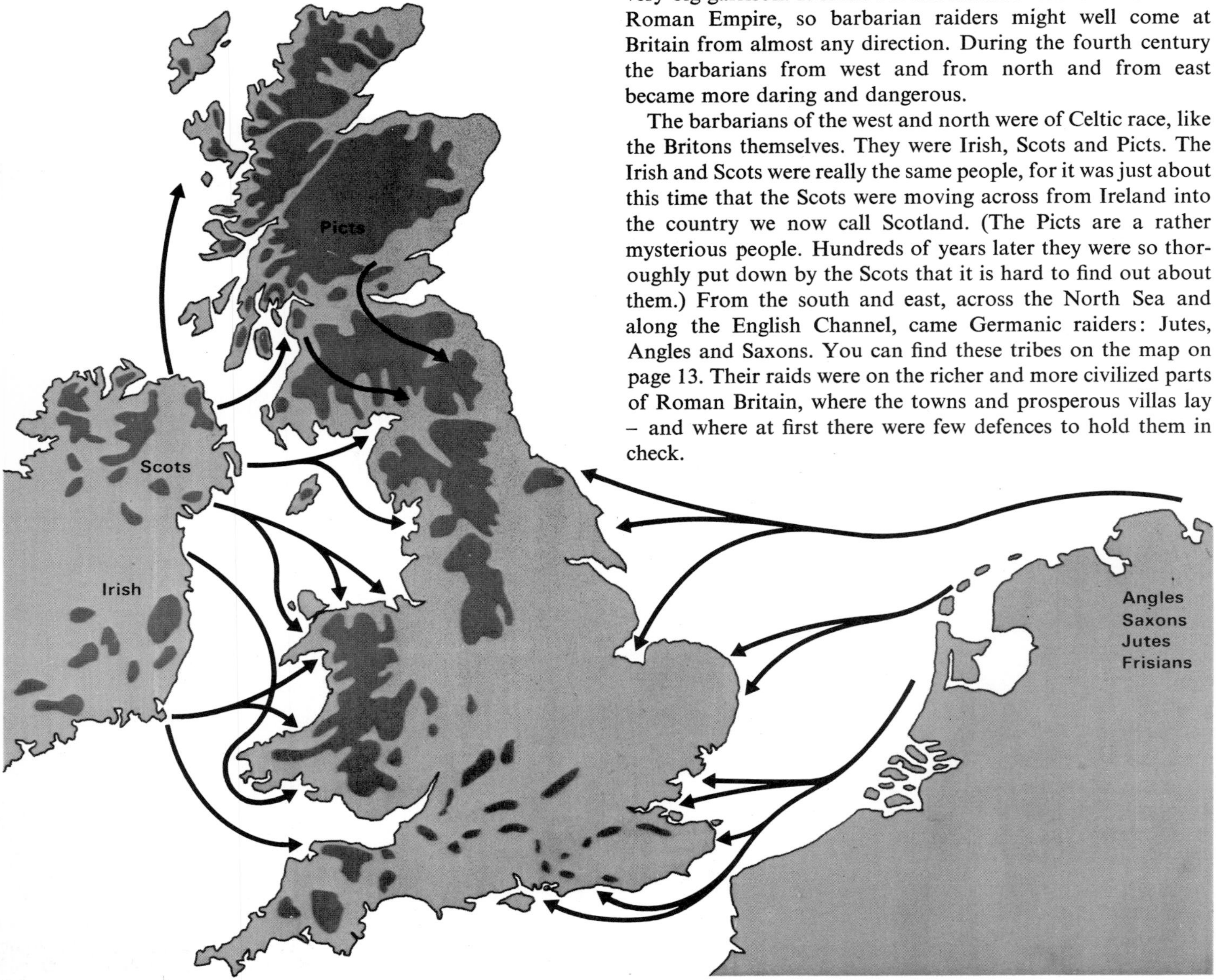

The end of Roman Britain: 'the Lost Centuries'

Roman Britain had always been a frontier province with a very big garrison. It stuck out northwards from the rest of the Roman Empire, so barbarian raiders might well come at Britain from almost any direction. During the fourth century the barbarians from west and from north and from east became more daring and dangerous.

The barbarians of the west and north were of Celtic race, like the Britons themselves. They were Irish, Scots and Picts. The Irish and Scots were really the same people, for it was just about this time that the Scots were moving across from Ireland into the country we now call Scotland. (The Picts are a rather mysterious people. Hundreds of years later they were so thoroughly put down by the Scots that it is hard to find out about them.) From the south and east, across the North Sea and along the English Channel, came Germanic raiders: Jutes, Angles and Saxons. You can find these tribes on the map on page 13. Their raids were on the richer and more civilized parts of Roman Britain, where the towns and prosperous villas lay – and where at first there were few defences to hold them in check.

Picts

Scots

Irish

Angles
Saxons
Jutes
Frisians

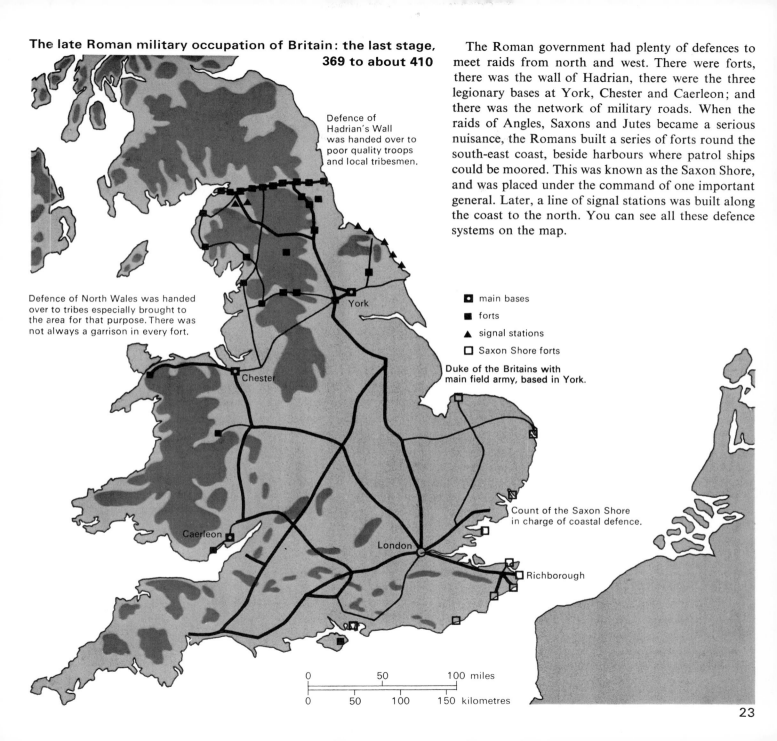

The late Roman military occupation of Britain: the last stage, 369 to about 410

Defence of Hadrian's Wall was handed over to poor quality troops and local tribesmen.

Defence of North Wales was handed over to tribes especially brought to the area for that purpose. There was not always a garrison in every fort.

York

Chester

Caerleon

London

Richborough

Duke of the Britains with main field army, based in York.

Count of the Saxon Shore in charge of coastal defence.

■ main bases
■ forts
▲ signal stations
□ Saxon Shore forts

The Roman government had plenty of defences to meet raids from north and west. There were forts, there was the wall of Hadrian, there were the three legionary bases at York, Chester and Caerleon; and there was the network of military roads. When the raids of Angles, Saxons and Jutes became a serious nuisance, the Romans built a series of forts round the south-east coast, beside harbours where patrol ships could be moored. This was known as the Saxon Shore, and was placed under the command of one important general. Later, a line of signal stations was built along the coast to the north. You can see all these defence systems on the map.

0   50   100 miles
0   50   100   150 kilometres

Richborough was the first Roman base in Britain, and the foundations of a monument to the landing in 43 can be seen on the right. When it became the centre of the Saxon Shore system the fort had to be enlarged. This meant filling in the ditches which you can see, re-excavated, in the foreground; and building new walls, remains of which stand in the background.

As you can see from this photograph, these forts were strong; but even the strongest walls and towers are useless without troops to man them. The signal stations, too, were well placed to give warning; but they were useless unless there was an army ready to march when the beacons were lit and the smoke-signals rose in the northern sky. And Roman Britain ran short of soldiers.

It sometimes happened that most of the army of Roman Britain was called to fight somewhere else, perhaps because its general was trying to make himself emperor. Also, there may have been in Britain, as there were in other parts of the Roman Empire, too few men who were willing to join the army. Anyway, it seems that about the year 380 the army handed over its old job of defending the north and west to the local British tribesmen. These Britons had never become very civilized. They had never taken to living in towns and villas, and had gone on living the hard life of mountain and moorland farmers. They seem to have been able to take care of themselves against Irish, Scots and Picts.

There still remained soldiers to guard the Saxon Shore, and to march north or west if the raids there became too strong for the local defenders. Then, in 406, the army in Britain began to set up its own emperors. One of these, Constantine III, took the army to Gaul and drove out some of the barbarians who had invaded that province. Just then the real emperor was in serious difficulties (page 16), but in 411 he was able to send a general who beat Constantine III and got the surviving British troops to join his own army. As for Britain, it would have to carry on without an army for a while.

For a while. That was the plan. In fact, the emperor's government was never able to send troops to Britain; you already know why. Britain was still part of the Roman Empire, but its people had to run their province for themselves.

We know very little about what happened next, so little that the years from about 400 to about 600 are sometimes called 'the Lost Centuries'. It seems likely that the Britons did quite well at first. It is true that there was not enough trade or surplus money to keep the towns in a very good state; for a while they seem to have done a useful job as markets, and then decayed. But there is no evidence that British towns were destroyed by barbarian attacks. Among the ruins that archaeologists have explored, the signs suggest that the buildings were neglected, then abandoned, and that they then fell into ruin. They were not burned down by an enemy.

Probably local chiefs in the north and west, and powerful landowners in the south and east, took over control in the districts where they lived. In the north and west the chiefs were strong enough to keep out the Irish, Scots and Picts, and eventually to set up kingdoms of their own. In the south and east the British leaders were not so lucky.

A Romano-British town
may have looked something like
this during the years of its decay.

Model of one of the coastal signal towers. This one stood on the Scarborough cliffs, and could send signals which could rapidly be passed to the base at York.

The English come to Britain

There is a famous story about how the first of the Germanic invaders settled in Britain. It is a very old story, and, though nobody can prove it to be true, it makes sense. It says that about 450 an important leader of the Britons, named Vortigern, needed soldiers to help him against his enemies. So he did what had often been done by the Romans: he hired barbarian warriors. He agreed with two Jute leaders, brothers called Hengist and Horsa, that they could live with their men in the island of Thanet if they would fight for him. After a while Vortigern and the brothers quarrelled. There was fighting, the Jutes won and soon they ruled over the whole of Kent.

That was the start. From then onwards Jute, Saxon and Angle pirates and raiders began to settle where they could.

Though these barbarian invaders were all very much the same people with the same language, and we tend to lump them together under the names of English or Saxons or Anglo-Saxons, they really belonged to the three distinct nations. The map shows you how the Jutes came first, taking the nearest good lands. Then came bands of Saxons, settling just beyond the Jutes or sailing up the rivers, deep into the country. When bands of Angles arrived, they had to go further north, again using the rivers.

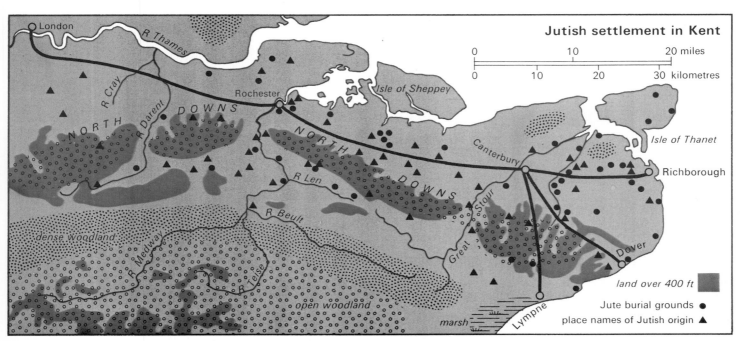

Jutish settlement in Kent

land over 400 ft ■
Jute burial grounds ●
place names of Jutish origin ▲

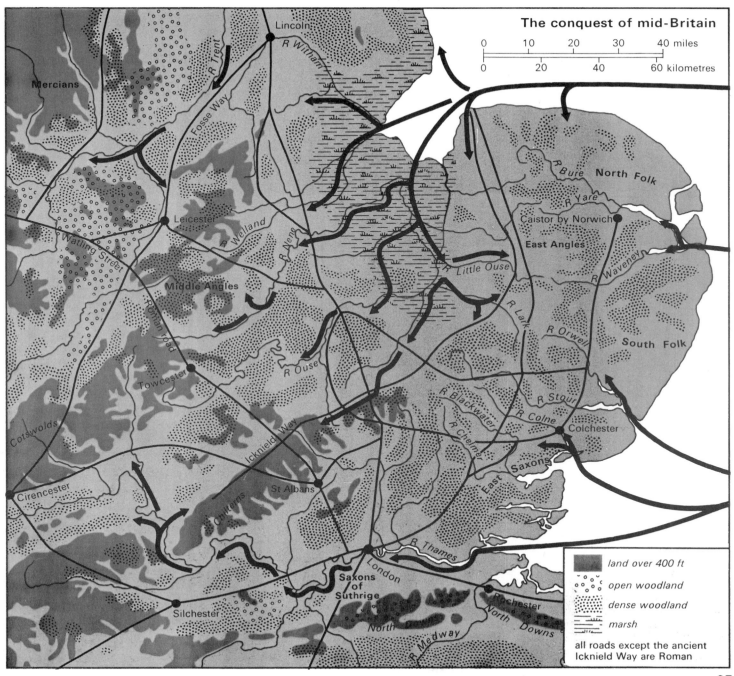

The conquest of mid-Britain

0   10   20   30   40 miles
0   20   40   60 kilometres

Mercians

R Trent

Lincoln

R Witham

Fosse Way

R Bure   North Folk

R Yare

Caistor by Norwich

East Angles

R Waveney

R Little Ouse

R Welland

R Nene

Leicester

Middle Angles

R Lark

R Orwell

South Folk

Watling Street

Roman Road

R Ouse

Towcester

R Blackwater

R Chelmer

R Stour

R Colne

Colchester

Cotswolds

Icknield Way

St Albans

Chilterns

East Saxons

Cirencester

London

R Thames

Saxons
of
Suthrige

Silchester

Rochester

North Downs

North

R Medway

land over 400 ft

open woodland

dense woodland

marsh

all roads except the ancient
Icknield Way are Roman

They came in boats like the one in the picture. Remains of such boats have been found both in North Germany and in England. Besides these 'war-canoes', the invaders may have had more bulky vessels to carry their families and animals and other belongings. Up the rivers they came, and on the rich, heavy soil of the valleys they built their wooden villages.

Almost anywhere in England you will find that the villages and towns have names given by the early English settlers. If you look up a dictionary of place-names to find out what the names in a district mean, you will probably find that most of them are Anglo-Saxon. Even where a place was first a Roman town or fort, the Anglo-Saxons have usually made some changes in the name; often they have added some such expression as 'chester' or 'cester' or 'caster', which was their version of the Latin word for a military camp, 'castra'. For their own settlements, they often ended the name with 'ham' (home) or 'ton' (township) or 'burgh' (stronghold). Some of the earliest settlements had names ending with '-ing', meaning 'his people'; for example, Worthing was the place where Worth lived with his family and servants.

Towns and villages are not the only signs on the map to remind us of the early English. As they settled, they formed themselves into kingdoms. This map shows the kingdoms, and some of the big districts inside the kingdoms. You might recognize a lot of county or shire names. The word 'shire' itself is Anglo-Saxon.

By the year 600 most of what had been Roman Britain was Anglo-Saxon England.

This ship was found buried at Nydam, in the region from which the Anglo-Saxons sailed to invade Britain. It is almost 75 ft (23 m) long and could carry about 40 men. The Sutton Hoo ship (p.8) was of similar design, though built two centuries later, and rather bigger and stronger.

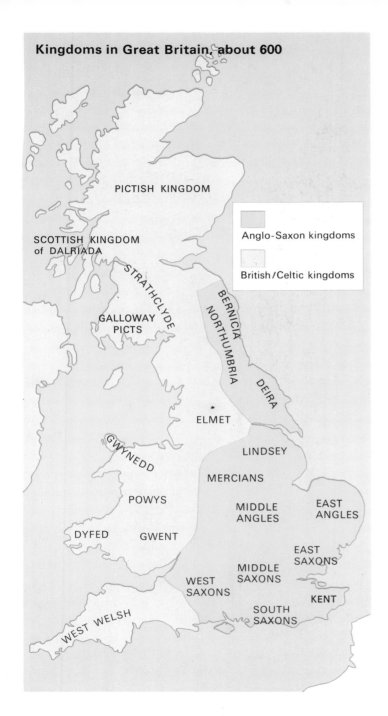

Kingdoms in Great Britain, about 600

PICTISH KINGDOM

SCOTTISH KINGDOM of DALRIADA

STRATHCLYDE

GALLOWAY PICTS

BERNICIA

NORTHUMBRIA

DEIRA

ELMET

GWYNEDD

LINDSEY

MERCIANS

POWYS

MIDDLE ANGLES

EAST ANGLES

DYFED

GWENT

EAST SAXONS

MIDDLE SAXONS

WEST SAXONS

KENT

SOUTH SAXONS

WEST WELSH

Anglo-Saxon kingdoms

British/Celtic kingdoms

About A.D. 500 the Anglo-Saxons liked to drink from graceful glasses made with a technical skill that suggests late Roman crafts-manship. They may have been imported from workshops on the Continent.

right: A claw beaker found in 1775 at Castle Eden, County Durham. It is 7·5 in. (190 mm) high.

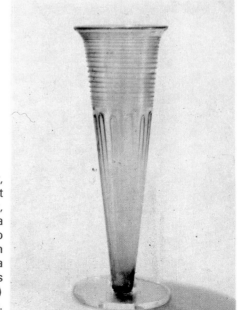

A cone beaker, found in 1863 at Kempston, Bedfordshire, in a grave which also contained golden ornaments and a toilet set. It is 10 in. (260 mm) high.

29

The long fight of the Britons

From what we have just learned, it does not look as though many Britons were left in the places where the English settled. It was different from what happened in France and Spain, as we saw on page 21. Probably the Britons fought until they were killed or driven away.

We know for certain that they fought hard, and sometimes won great victories over the English. Behind all the doubtful stories and legends, we can be fairly sure that the Britons had two great war-leaders. One was Ambrosius Aurelianus, 'the last of the Romans', as he was called. After him came Artorius, whom most people know as King Arthur.

Pictures of Arthur and his men usually show them dressed in the sort of armour which was not used for another thousand years. Most of the stories about them are probably just as untrue. It seems most likely that in fact Arthur's 'knights' were heavy mail-clad cavalrymen; such soldiers had been used by the Romans before the Western Empire had collapsed, and were still being used in the Eastern Empire. Arthur is thought to have won a great victory at a place called Mount Badon, somewhere in south-west Britain, which put a stop to the advance of the English for half a century, from about 500 until after 550.

After Arthur, however, there seem to have been no more men who could lead the Britons to victory. Perhaps, too, there were no more trained cavalrymen or horses big enough to carry them. According to what some of the old British priests wrote, the British chiefs were too fond of getting drunk and fighting each other. So the English came on again.

left: King Arthur slaying Mordred, according to a fifteenth-century Netherlands artist. He imagined them in armour of his own time, when many Arthurian tales were being written. People have continued to picture Arthur in this fashion, but he probably looked more like the drawing below.

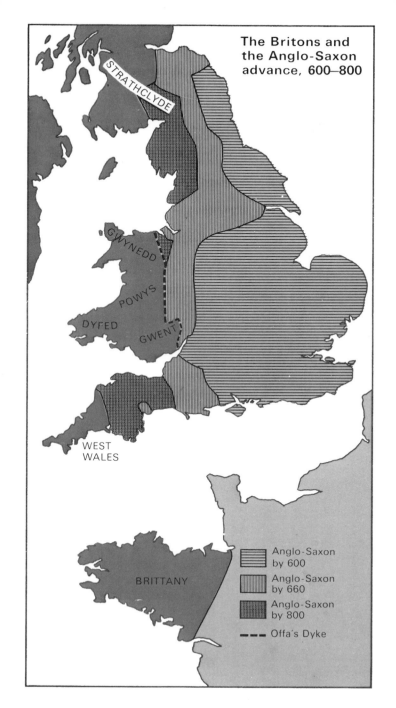

The Britons and the Anglo-Saxon advance, 600–800

STRATHCLYDE

GWYNEDD

POWYS

DYFED

GWENT

WEST WALES

BRITTANY

Anglo-Saxon by 600

Anglo-Saxon by 660

Anglo-Saxon by 800

--- Offa's Dyke

This photograph of part of Offa's Dyke was taken near Llanfair Waterdine, Shropshire, looking north-west.

This map shows you the result. The Britons were left with three separate areas: Strathclyde in the north, Wales and Cornwall. Some of them had crossed the Channel to the western tip of France, which is still called Brittany and where the people have their own Breton language which is very like Welsh.

In Wales the Britons held out so well that at last, about 790, King Offa of Mercia, who was then the most powerful English king, had a great earthwork made from Liverpool Bay to the Bristol Channel, to mark the frontier between Welsh and English. Offa's Dyke can still be seen. Beyond it, the Welsh now had a chance to regain their strength after their long struggle. But still their chiefs could not agree. The Britons, or Welsh, as we had better call them from this time on, never became a united nation.

As for this name 'Welsh', it is an Anglo-Saxon word meaning 'foreigner, alien'. This was the name given to the last of the Britons in the land that had once been theirs.

Life in the English villages

You often see in books pictures of English villages, rather like the picture of a barbarian village on page 6 of this book. It is worth while trying to get a picture of such a village, because almost all the English lived in little settlements of this sort, taking most of what they needed from the forest and fields and rivers. Unfortunately these pictures are bound to be mostly guesses. We know far less about what an English village looked like than we do about a Roman town or villa. There are good reasons for this.

Firstly, the English built in wood, hardly ever in stone. So, except for a few marks left in the soil where the wooden posts have rotted, there is little for the archaeologist to work on.

Then, in most places, it is not possible for the archaeologist to look for even these slight traces, because modern towns and villages have been built on the same sites as the Anglo-Saxon settlements. The places have never been deserted, as so many Roman places were.

Finally, the Anglo-Saxons themselves have left no pictures or clear descriptions of their dwellings; and those writings which have come down to us from Anglo-Saxon times were written many hundreds of years after the English came to settle in Britain.

So you see how difficult it is to find out for certain what an Anglo-Saxon village was like. We have to do our best with those remains which have been discovered, and use our common sense. After this warning, we can try to build up our own picture of what an English village was like about the year 600. If we make a list of the things which must almost certainly have been there, we can then try to put the pieces together.

Land and water

To begin with, there is the countryside itself. If you were an English settler picking a good site you would surely want to be near woods, so as to get building timber, firewood, acorns for the pigs; and to be able to hunt woodland animals. Most of England was then very thickly wooded, so there would be no difficulty so far. If you had much choice, you would probably pick a fairly open stretch of land, which would not need too much clearing, near the edge of a forest.

You would also need water. A small stream might be enough. A river would be useful if you wished to travel by boat, but it might also bring unwelcome visitors. A river would give better fishing, and if there were marshes nearby there might be wild fowl.

There is much to be considered, quite apart from things like the quality of the soil, which will not show in a picture. Here is one imaginary site; you can invent your own. Or perhaps you know a modern town or village which was founded in Anglo-Saxon times, and can make a good guess about what the landscape was like then.

Fields

Now, before you think of the building of the settlement itself, there is the very important question of how the fields should be laid out. We cannot be perfectly sure, but it seems very likely that the English brought with them a method of laying out the land which is known as the 'open field' system.

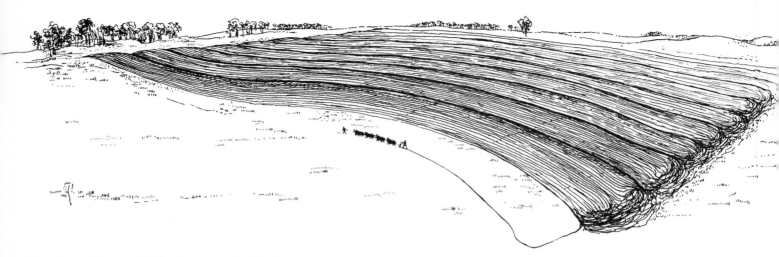

Plowing with an eight-ox team, probably the oxen of three or four families combined. The strips would become humped in the middle as the plow heaped the earth inwards. It has been suggested that even on level ground an ox-team would not make a perfectly straight strip, because they gradually prepared to turn before they reached the end. In practice the size and shape of strips would vary according to the ground, and perhaps the strength of the team.

below: Ridge-and-furrow patterns left on present-day fields by earlier plowing near Padbury, Buckinghamshire.

The first thing about it was that the land was plowed in strips, long and thin. If you think about it, this is the most sensible way to plow, as the diagram above shows. A farmer wanted to be able to drive his oxen and plow straight, without wasting time and having the trouble of turning round more than he had to. If you watch a farmer nowadays, you will see that it is still true; but today the farmer uses a tractor, which does not have to pause for breath at the end of the furrow. When an Anglo-Saxon was marking out the land, he would probably try to make each strip just about big enough for a team of oxen to plow in a day, and the distance the oxen could go without a pause was a 'furrow-long' or furlong. This sort of plowing in strips went on for many hundreds of years after the Anglo-Saxons, and you can still sometimes see the ridge pattern which is left on fields now used as pasture.

34

above: So-called Celtic fields, Burderop Down, Wiltshire.

above right: Part of the South Field at Laxton, Nottinghamshire, where open-field methods have survived. The photograph gives some idea of the expanse of such fields.

The Britons seem to have preferred smallish, square fields; they probably practised criss-cross plowing and often, anyway, they farmed on the lighter soils of the hillsides, where there was not room for really big fields. The English preferred to arrange all the strips needed by the villagers in two or three vast fields. Sometimes air photographs can still show us, in places where the ground has not been too much worked and built over since, the pattern of these different sorts of fields.

You would need in each field enough plow-land for every family in your village. This would mean a lot of strips. They would probably be shared out as this diagram shows, so that each farmer would have strips in all parts of the field, which seems fair. We know that this happened hundreds of years later, when open fields were still being used, and it seems likely that it happened so from the start.

below: Diagram of one family's share in one field. You can work out how many families probably lived in this village, and about how many acres they needed.

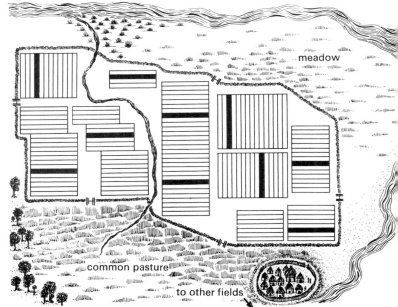

meadow

common pasture

to other fields

Two and three field crop rotation systems

2 field

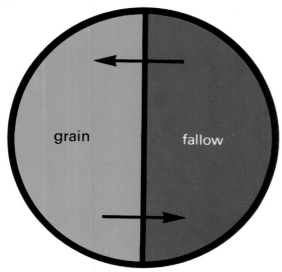

3 field

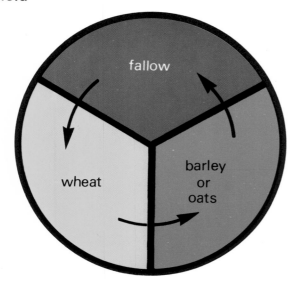

But why not just one big field? Why have two or three? The reason was that the land had to be given a rest every two or three years, so that it could get back some of the goodness which the crops had taken out of it. If the village had two fields, one would have a rest (or lie fallow, to use the correct term) while the other grew crops, and there would be an exchange every year. But since different crops were known to take different times to grow, and, as we know nowadays, they take different things from the soil, it was found possible to arrange the land so that only one-third was fallow each year. This meant using three fields and changing round the crops as the diagram on the left shows.

The open field method of farming seems to have been used in most parts of England where the ground was suitable, though the Jutes did not use it. So you will be safe enough if you put open fields into your picture of a village. Take care to make them big enough.

Pasture and meadow

We have now thought of a number of ways of getting food: hunting, fishing, growing crops for bread. But, apart from the pigs, eating acorns in the wood, our animals have been neglected. The cows, oxen and sheep – horses were scarce and expensive in those days – need grassland for pasture. There is also the problem of keeping some of the animals alive during the winter. This means hay, and the hay is grown in a meadow. Only the best animals can be kept; the rest have to be slaughtered in the autumn and winter.

The houses

Now we can think about shelter. There must be a fence or stockade to keep out wild animals, and perhaps outlaws and enemies. Inside would be the houses and sheds of the villagers. On the right is a plan taken from a village which has been excavated, and some ideas that historians have had about the houses which the early English may have lived in. In different places the settlers would use whatever materials seemed best – wood, stones, clay, straw; but since this would depend on the place, probably all the buildings in any one village would be made in the same way.

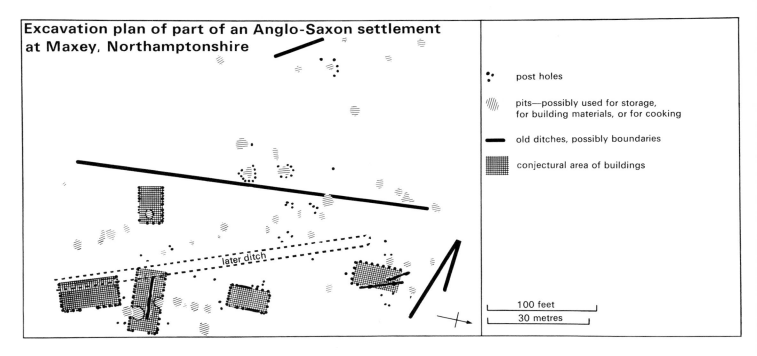

Excavation plan of part of an Anglo-Saxon settlement at Maxey, Northamptonshire

later ditch

:. post holes

pits—possibly used for storage, for building materials, or for cooking

old ditches, possibly boundaries

conjectural area of buildings

100 feet

30 metres

The archaeologist has no stone remains to help him now. He must examine the ground carefully for every change in colour and texture which tells that there was once a hole of some sort, and decide what sort of hole it was. Then — he hopes — the dots on his plan will fall into a pattern, as they have done here.

left: In the Anglo-Saxon village at Sutton Courtenay, Berkshire, some homes consisted of two or three small huts placed close together. This reconstruction drawing shows one of the better houses of the village. The small hut in front may have been the kitchen. The other two were linked at the corner.

37

The hall

You must now decide whether or not your village has an important chief, or even a king, living in it. Such a great man, of course, would need his hall, the sort of place we mentioned on page 10. Though there are no good Anglo-Saxon pictures of halls, and so far the archaeologists have not been able to help much, there are descriptions. We know from the epic poem of 'Beowulf' what a king's hall was like: the porch, the high roof, the carved beams, the hearth down the centre, the tables round the walls. Fine large buildings can be made of wood, as you can see from the picture below, and probably methods of building in wood did not change much between the English invasion and the time when this barn was built. If you can imagine a great room like this, but with the timbers richly carved and painted, you will have an idea of the inside of the hall. In your picture of the settlement only the outside will show, but do not forget the outbuildings belonging to the hall, the stables and huts for animals and slaves.

The people

The village is almost complete. There may be a water-mill, but most probably the English had to grind their corn by hand. No shops. Perhaps a smithy. No church, of course. All we need now are the people.

From graves, archaeologists can tell us about their skeletons and the metal things they used and wore, but the clothes have perished. It seems that their garments were simple. Women wore long dresses, men tunics and leggings; there were big cloaks for bad weather. Clothes would be made of wool, leather and possibly linen. Brooches were needed to fasten them. Details like this, though, will not show in a picture of a whole village.

Now you know practically all the important things that anyone knows about what an early English village looked like; quite enough, certainly, for you to make your own picture of one.

Godmersham barn, in Kent, is a fifteenth-century structure, but the beam work may well resemble the construction of an Anglo-Saxon hall.

The price of life

You hardly need to be told that in your village there was plenty of hard work and not much comfort. There was danger, too. If a family lost its grown-up men, the women and children and old people might find it difficult to stay alive without their workers and fighters.

As you saw on page 10, there was a system of compensation. If one man killed another, he would have to pay the dead man's price to the bereaved family and lord. (This was for straightforward killing; murder was underhand, secret killing, and a murderer was killed himself if he could be found out.)

Many years after the invasions, the laws of many English kingdoms were written down, and they give us the 'price lists' of different kingdoms at different times. A man's price was his 'wergild', and you can see on this table how the prices varied. Noblemen, chiefs or members of the king's band of chosen warriors, could cost as much as six times an ordinary man, or churl.

You may think that killers were let off very easily in, say, Kent in the seventh century, where an ordinary man's wergild was only 100 shillings. But in those days you could buy a great deal with 100 shillings, as the sketch below tells you. When you think that a churl was quite well off if he owned a team of four oxen, you will realize that killing other people was very expensive.

Most crimes, like killings, were punished by fines. It was a

TABLE OF WERGILDS

KENT early seventh century

| Nobleman | 300 golden shillings |
| Peasant | 100 golden shillings |

Each golden shilling was worth about 50 cents

WESSEX late seventh century

Nobleman	1,200 shillings
Lesser nobleman	600 shillings
Peasant	200 shillings

Each shilling was worth about 12 cents

NORTHUMBRIA tenth century

King	30,000 thrymsas
Archbishop or Prince	15,000 thrymsas
Bishop or Ealdorman	8,000 thrymsas
High Reeve or Hold	4,000 thrymsas
Priest or Thegn	2,000 thrymsas
Peasant	266 thrymsas

Each thrymsa was worth about 8 cents

London prices, early tenth century:
ox, 75 cents; cow, 50 cents; pig, 25 cents; sheep, 12 cents.

good idea, as the money went to the people who had suffered the loss. Anyway, there were no prisons.

There were no police, either. Anybody who had been wronged had to come forward at the moot (you heard about that on page 6) and accuse the wrong-doer.

100 sheep

39

ACCUSATION

Often there could be no argument. In a village, most people would have a pretty good idea of what was going on, and a guilty man would confess and pay up. If there were to be an argument, the accused man would try to find men of good reputation to swear that they believed he was telling the truth. These men were his 'oath-helpers'. You may think that it sounds as though it would be easy to get away with crimes. But you must remember that everybody knew everybody else, and nobody wanted to be known as a liar or a fool.

Just as a man's wergild depended on whether he was noble or churl, so did the value of his oath. A nobleman's oath counted for more; but he had more to lose.

Sometimes a man would be condemned to pay a fine which was too much for him to raise, even with the help of his family and lord. He now had a hard choice. He could allow himself to be sold as a slave, and thus pay the fine while he lost his liberty. Or he could run away. If he fled, he became an outlaw, outside the law. Anyone else was entitled to kill him, as if he were a wolf or some other dangerous beast. In fact, a stranger who could not give a good account of himself, or who seemed to have something to hide, ran a risk of being treated as an outlaw. Honest travellers who were journeying through woods were supposed to shout and blow their horns, to let everyone know that they were coming; men travelling silently were most likely to be outlaws.

All this was very makeshift, when you compare it with the laws and courts of the Romans. England was a wild land. Even with lords, families and moots, it was safest for a man to have a strong right arm and a stout spear.

OATH HELPING

The Christian church

About a hundred years before the barbarians had begun to settle in the Roman Empire, an emperor had become Christian. His name was Constantine, and in 313 he ordered that Christians should no longer be persecuted. Soon, Christianity became the religion of most of the people in the Roman Empire, both Eastern and Western.

Bishops

All over the Empire, churches were built in the towns and cities. Those in the cities were usually built in the same way as the basilicas. The basilica was the 'town hall' which stood at one side of the forum, and where the judges used to hear cases. In the Christian churches, there were altars and priests instead of judges, but the buildings were often alike, as you can see from these pictures.

Just as the Roman Empire itself was very carefully ruled, with officials and governors in the towns and provinces, so the church was organized. In every important city there was an important man known as 'episcopus' or bishop, who had to look after the Christians and their priests in the city and the countryside around. The bishop would have his 'cathedra' or throne in the main church of the city, and thus the main church was called a cathedral. The greatest cities had especially important bishops, who were often called 'patriarchs' or ruling fathers. Both Rome and Constantinople, the chief cities of the Western and Eastern Empires respectively, had very powerful patriarchs.

So, by the time the barbarians came, the whole of the Roman Empire was Christian, and every big town had its bishop.

above: A reconstruction drawing of the early second-century Basilica Ulpia, Rome. It was common for a basilica to have at one end a rounded projection, or apse, in which the magistrate's chair was placed. Christians used the same place for the bishop's 'cathedra' (see page 57).

below: The church of St Maria Maggiore, Rome, is a basilica built in the fourth century, rebuilt in the fifth, and much embellished since.

The Christian barbarians

The bishops stayed at their posts. They and other Christians tried to teach the barbarian conquerors the new religion. The bishops were often the most important men remaining in the cities, and so they had a lot to do with the barbarian chiefs, and could speak to them about Christianity. Gradually, one after another, the barbarian peoples became Christians. For some years, many of the tribes preferred a type of Christianity called Arianism, which said that Jesus Christ was the Son of God but not so important as his Father. Eventually, though, the Arian religion died out, and all the tribes that had settled in the Western Roman Empire accepted the same ideas as the bishop of Rome.

Even though Rome no longer was the home of a mighty emperor with legions at his command, this city was still the most important place in the west. Nobody, not even a barbarian, could forget Rome's tremendous history, and all that Rome had made. Once a barbarian chief, fighting in Italy against an army of the eastern emperor, was outwitted by the enemy general, so that he would have to retreat from the city of Rome, which he had been holding. The barbarian was furious and swore that he would destroy Rome before he went. The eastern emperor's general heard of this, and he sent a letter to the barbarian. In it, he appealed to him to spare Rome, and asked the barbarian if he wished to be remembered as the man who destroyed the greatest city in the world. The barbarian retreated without harming the city.

The Pope

When there was no emperor in Rome, the bishop soon became the most important man. Someone had to protect and keep order in the city, and the bishop did it. You saw on page 18 how one bishop of Rome had saved the city from Attila, and you may remember the special title he had: Pope, which means father. The other bishops in the west, those in Italy, France, Spain and Africa, came to look on the Pope as their leader. At the same time, the bishops of the Eastern Empire took their lead from the emperor in Constantinople and his patriarch.

So in both the Eastern Roman Empire and what had been the Western Empire Christianity had won. All those people belonged to the same universal (or 'catholic') church. In the

west the Pope led, in the east the patriarch of Constantinople, who obeyed the eastern emperor. Obviously there was the danger of trouble between the two parts, but so far it was all one church.

Hermits and monks

As you have seen, the bishops were important men, dealing with kings, chiefs, generals and emperors. They were kept very busy, trying to make their church grow safer and stronger.

But there were some Christians who did not wish to have anything to do with what went on in cities and at the courts of kings. They thought that in such places men became bad, that they tried to become powerful and rich, and so were always being tempted to be greedy, ambitious, mean, selfish and cruel, caring only for themselves and trying to beat everyone else. Some Christians who thought this way preferred to go away from it all, to cut themselves off from a world of selfishness and wickedness and to spend their time praying to God.

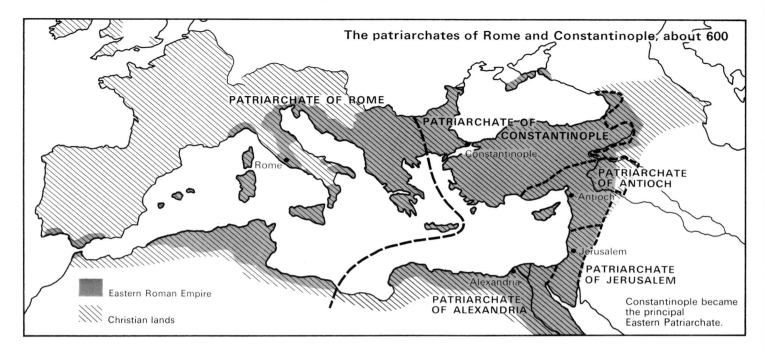

The patriarchates of Rome and Constantinople, about 600

PATRIARCHATE OF ROME

PATRIARCHATE OF CONSTANTINOPLE

Constantinople

PATRIARCHATE OF ANTIOCH

Antioch

Rome

Jerusalem

PATRIARCHATE OF JERUSALEM

Alexandria

PATRIARCHATE OF ALEXANDRIA

Constantinople became the principal Eastern Patriarchate.

■ Eastern Roman Empire

⧄ Christian lands

Such men and women became hermits. There were many, for instance, in Egypt, who lived in huts in the desert among the rocks, entirely alone except when they went to church. It is said that about the year 325 there were over 5,000 of them in only one part of the desert. Many of these hermits were so anxious to be free from any desire for comfort that they walled themselves into tombs, or spent their lives sitting on the tops of huge pillars, receiving only the smallest possible amount of food and drink.

Others preferred to live in groups, so that they could help each other in praying, or studying the Bible, or working. Men who did this were called monks; women, nuns. A hermit could do exactly as he himself chose, but a monk had to fit in with the other monks in his group. Whenever people live and work in groups there have to be rules, so each monastery or nunnery would have a set of rules which the monks and nuns had agreed to obey. These rules would be made by their leader.

left: Bishop Wulfila translated the Arian version of the Gospel into Gothic. This copy, in silver ink on purple parchment, was made in Italy about 500.

Benedict and the Rule

These ideas spread wherever Christianity was strong. From the east they moved to the west, and many noble and intelligent men became monks. One of the greatest was St Benedict.

Benedict was born in Nursia, in central Italy, about 480, and his family was rich. When he was seventeen he decided to be a hermit, and went to live in the mountains near Subiaco. He was not allowed to remain a hermit for long. Other people heard how good he was, and asked to be allowed to come and live with him, as monks. He agreed, and organized twelve groups of monks who were to live as he ordered. He had difficulties. Some monks at times so disliked his ideas that they tried to kill him. About 520 he left Subiaco and went south, to Cassino, where he founded a new monastery. Here he spent the rest of his life. Meanwhile Italy became a battlefield where the Goths and the armies of the eastern emperor fought a long

and savage war which neither side was strong enough to win. While this futile and cruel war was turning one part of Italy after another into a ravaged ruin, Benedict was working at Cassino, where he died about 555. The kings and generals left behind them a wasted land. Benedict left his famous 'Rule'.

The Rule of Benedict ordered that each monk should take vows of Poverty and Obedience. That is, he had to give up all his belongings and submit to the orders of his abbot (the title of the head of a monastery). At Cassino Benedict also made new monks promise to remain in the monastery all their lives. A monk had to dress simply in a long black tunic, with a hood, or cowl as it is generally called. He must never eat meat. The monk was allowed about eight hours' sleep, and the rest of his time every day was divided between services in the monastery church or chapel, working, and reading the Scriptures. The Rule explained clearly how the day should be divided, and how the monastery should be run. As for the abbot, he had complete power over the whole monastery, and he was expected to use his power wisely.

This Rule was so practical, worked so well, that monastery after monastery decided to follow it, until it became the main rule for monasteries all over Europe for the next thousand years. During much of that time the monasteries were to be the most civilized and peaceful places in all Europe.

St Benedict giving the Rule to his monks. A modern picture based on an eighth-century representation.

below: After fourteen centuries of growth and rebuilding, St Benedict's monastery on Monte Cassino looked like this. Because of its dominating position it became the centre of heavy fighting during the Second World War, and was destroyed. A new monastery has been erected on the old site.

Christianity in Britain

Christianity in Roman Britain

Britain was part of the Roman Empire when it became Christian. Constantine himself was in Britain when he was proclaimed emperor, and there is a legend that his mother, Helena, was a Christian and a Briton. Before the time of Constantine some Christians had been martyred in Britain, the best known of them being St Alban. Now Christians could worship freely, and the religion seems to have become very strong in Britain.

Archaeologists have found some signs of Christianity. Buildings which seem to have been churches have been found in two Romano-British towns, Silchester and Caerwent. The deliberate destruction of a temple of Mithras at Carrawburgh, on Hadrian's Wall, looks more like the work of Christians putting an end to the worship of a false god than either a barbarian raid or gradual decay. In the villa at Lullingstone, in Kent, there was a chapel with Christian pictures on the walls, and this mosaic of Christ was found in a villa at Hinton St Mary, in Dorset.

Christianity reaches Ireland

From Roman Britain, Christianity spread to the Irish. A young Briton with the very Roman name of Patricius was kidnapped by Irish pirates and sold in Ireland as a slave. Patrick, as he is usually called, escaped to Gaul after six years. He became a monk and eighteen years later, in 432, he returned to Ireland as a missionary. He was amazingly successful. When he died in 461 Ireland was a Christian country.

Irish monks and monasteries

The new religion swept through Ireland like a fire, and many Irish gave themselves up to it completely. They became monks. During the hundred years after Patrick's death, the Irish covered their land with monasteries and nunneries. These had nothing to do with the ideas of St Benedict – indeed, many of them were founded before he was born. Life in an Irish monastery was not only disciplined and simple; it was almost savage in its hardness. Irish monks and nuns were almost as stern with themselves as the hermits of Egypt had been.

Fourth-century portrait of Christ found at Hinton St Mary.

left: Skellig Michael, off the coast of County Kerry. Irish monks made a monastery here.

below left: Some of the monks' huts on Skellig Michael.

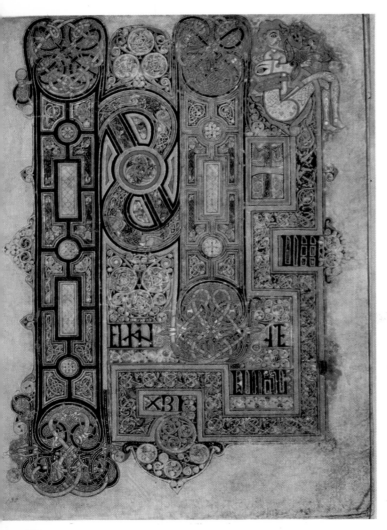

The Book of Kells was probably written in Ireland about 730. This page is the beginning of the Gospel of St Mark. It measures 13×9·875 in. (330×250 mm).

The monasteries themselves were no more than groups of little stone or wood huts, with a chapel, a kitchen and a larger hut for eating. Like Benedict's monks, the Irish ate no meat; but they went further – they had only one meal a day. Like Benedict's monks, the Irish spent much time praying; but some of them kept their arms stretched out, like a cross, all the time they were at prayer, or stood up to their necks in a cold river. If Benedict's monks broke the Rule they were punished, but not by the severe floggings which were quite normal in Irish monasteries.

These Irish monks, however, were neither madmen nor savages. They showed great kindness to the sick and the poor and seem to have been very fond of animals. They studied Latin carefully, in order to read the Scriptures well, and so they became the best educated men in Europe. They copied the Scriptures, and decorated them with designs and colours of delicate and splendid beauty.

About a century after the death of St Patrick, these astonishing monks began to wander. The map shows you where Irish monks are known to have been. Some may have sailed westwards and been lost in the waters of the ocean; their boats were probably small and frail. Those who met heathens set about teaching them Christianity. Those who sailed to Christian lands brought with them, wherever they went, their burning enthusiasm for learning and for the Christian religion.

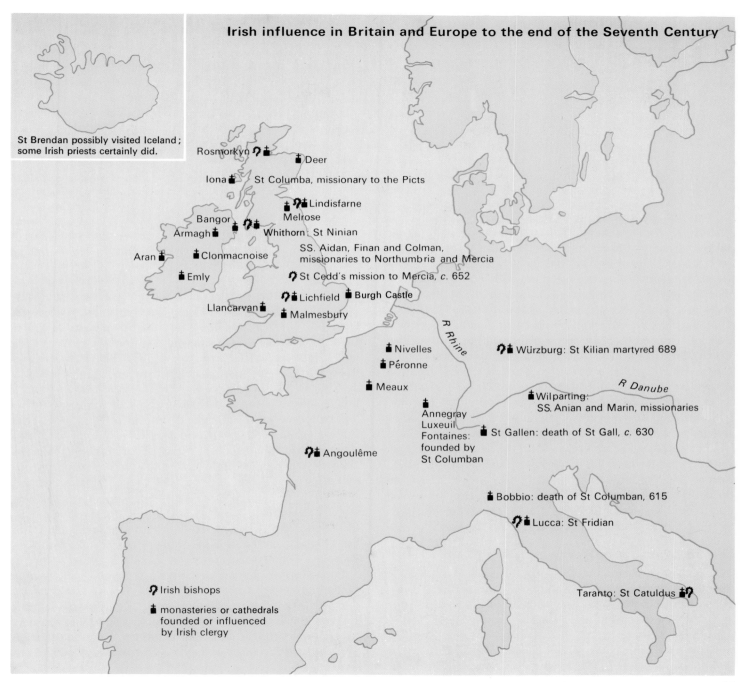

Irish influence in Britain and Europe to the end of the Seventh Century

St Brendan possibly visited Iceland;
some Irish priests certainly did.

Rosmorkyn
Deer
Iona — St Columba, missionary to the Picts
Lindisfarne
Melrose
Bangor
Armagh
Whithorn: St Ninian
Aran
Clonmacnoise
SS. Aidan, Finan and Colman,
missionaries to Northumbria and Mercia
Emly
St Cedd's mission to Mercia, c. 652
Lichfield   Burgh Castle
Llancarvan
Malmesbury

Nivelles
Péronne
Würzburg: St Kilian martyred 689
Meaux
Wilparting:
SS. Anian and Marin, missionaries
Annegray
Luxeuil
Fontaines:
founded by
St Columban
St Gallen: death of St Gall, c. 630
Angoulême

R Rhine
R Danube

Bobbio: death of St Columban, 615
Lucca: St Fridian

Taranto: St Catuldus

ϟ Irish bishops
✝ monasteries or cathedrals
founded or influenced
by Irish clergy

49

The conversion of the English

In the rest of Britain, things were going badly for the Christians; the heathen English were winning. Among the Britons there were many holy men, some of them wandering Irish monks. If you look at a modern map of Wales you will see many places with names beginning with 'Llan', and each of these is supposed to be where a saint paused and built a chapel. But it seems that none of these saints tried to teach Christianity to the English. Probably the Britons hated the English so much that they wanted them to go on being heathen, so that they would all burn for ever in Hell after they died. Anyway, the English would probably have thought that a priest from the Britons was some sort of bad magician, and killed him without delay.

So the English went on worshipping their own gods, whose names we still use for the days of the week: Tiw, Woden, Thunor and the goddess Freya. Of all the barbarians who had settled in the lands of the Western Roman Empire, the Anglo-Saxons had the reputation of being the fiercest. They were certainly fierce enough to fight among themselves very often, and to sell one another as slaves. It was because of this, so the story goes, that Christianity at last reached the English.

The mission from Rome

You must have heard the story of the Roman monk and the English children who were being sold in the market at Rome. He thought that they did not look at all like devilish savages, and that it was a great pity that such people should not be Christians. Years later the monk, Gregory, became Pope. He was such an important Pope that he is known as Gregory the Great. In spite of all his other work, he remembered that the English were still heathen. In 596 he ordered a party of monks, led by one called Augustine, to go and teach the English.

These monks were very unhappy about their job. Our earliest book about all this, written just over a hundred years after it happened, says they were 'on their journey seized with a sudden fear, and began to think of returning home, rather than proceed to a barbarous, fierce and unbelieving nation, to whose very language they were strangers'. But the Pope was firm. He ordered Augustine to go on, though he asked the bishops of the Franks to help him, and to send interpreters with him across the English Channel.

If Augustine feared the English, Ethelbert was rather nervous about the monks. He was afraid that they might work magic spells on him. Because magicians were supposed to find it harder to work out of doors, the king met the monks in the open. When he met them, though, Ethelbert thought that these monks from Rome were good men who only wished to do good to him and his people. He allowed them to come and live in the royal town of Canterbury, while he made up his mind about whether he ought to become a Christian himself.

Here again Augustine was lucky. The people of Kent were more civilized than the other English. Canterbury had once been a Roman town, and some of the Roman buildings were still being used. There was even a church, which the queen used; it is still there, though it has been altered since those days. Here Augustine and his monks settled, and after a while King Ethelbert decided that he would accept their religion. Where the king led, the nobles and ordinary people followed. Kent became a Christian kingdom.

Pope Gregory made Augustine an archbishop. He was the first archbishop of Canterbury.

It was a good start. Though small, Kent was richer than most of the English kingdoms, and Ethelbert was respected by the other English kings. All the same, Augustine found it difficult to spread Christianity any further. The other kings were suspicious. King Redwald of the East Angles tried to be

ECCLESIASTICAE GENTIS ANGLORVM

An initial from a copy of Bede's *Historia Ecclesiastica Gentis Anglorum* (Ecclesiastical History of the English People) which was probably made in Bede's own monastery about the time he died. Though a later writer has put Augustine's name round the head, scholars believe that this is a portrait of Gregory, because the cross and book were often used as symbols of the Pope. The portrait is only 1·5 in. (40 mm) high.

safe; he built a special temple with one side for the old gods and the other for the new Christian God. The other kings would not even go as far as that.

Augustine also failed when he tried to make friends with the British bishops of Wales. They suspected him of wanting to come and be their chief. They had been working alone for a long time, without the help or the interference of anyone from Rome, and they preferred to go on like that.

Even in Kent itself things began to go wrong. After both Ethelbert and Augustine died, the new king himself went back to the old gods; but this did not last for long.

So more than twenty years went by. Christianity was established in Kent. Then it made a sudden leap to the other end of England.

Roman monks in Northumbria

The kingdom of Northumbria was made up of two smaller kingdoms: Bernicia and Deira, and sometimes included Lindsey to the south. It covered a lot of ground, but was not rich. The Northumbrians were warlike. They were feared and hated by the Britons of Wales and Strathclyde, and respected by the other English. King Edwin of Northumbria wished to marry a Kentish princess. She agreed, but only if she could have Christian priests with her. History seemed to be repeating itself.

The leader of these priests was called Paulinus. He soon made King Edwin begin to think that the Christians might be right, after all. In 627 Edwin decided to discuss it with his chief men. So they listened while Paulinus explained what Christians believed, and they began to think that this made more sense than what they had believed before. Even the chief of the heathen priests thought so. One noble put it like this:

'The present life of man, O king, seems to me, in comparison of that time which is unknown to us, like to the swift flight of a sparrow through the room wherein you sit at supper in winter, with your commanders and ministers, and a good fire in the midst, whilst the storms of rain and snow prevail abroad; the sparrow, I say, flying in at one door, and immediately out at another, whilst he is within, is safe from the wintry storm; but after a short space of fair weather, he immediately vanishes out of your sight, into the dark winter from which he had emerged. So the life of man appears for a short space, but of what went before, or what is to follow, we are utterly ignorant. If, therefore, this new doctrine contains something more certain, it seems justly to deserve to be followed.'

After this, Paulinus and his helpers were kept busy every day from dawn to nightfall, teaching and baptizing the Northumbrians.

The new faith of Northumbria was soon to be tested.

There came against King Edwin two strong enemies: Penda, leader of the heathen Mercians, and the British prince Cadwallon, from North Wales. Late in 632 there was a great battle at Heathfield. Edwin was killed, his warriors scattered. Northumbria was defenceless before her enemies.

Cadwallon the Briton was master now. He slew two Northumbrian princes who tried to make themselves kings, and slaughtered the people without mercy. Being a Briton, he was a Christian, but it made no difference. You can understand

Christianity leaps North, 625–32

Roman church

*Celtic church
(British and Irish)*

PICTISH KINGDOM

SCOTTISH KINGDOM of DALRIADA

STRATHCLYDE

GALLOWAY PICTS

KINGDOMS OF IRELAND

BERNICIA

Yeavering

NORTHUMBRIA

DEIRA

York

Paulinus' mission to Northumbria

LINDSEY

Lincoln

Heathen English Kingdoms

WELSH (BRITISH) KINGDOMS

KENT

Canterbury

how it was that many Northumbrians thought that the Christian God had forsaken them, and began once more to worship the old gods.

Paulinus fled. He went back to Kent with the queen. One of his helpers, James the Deacon, bravely remained in York, trying to keep Christianity alive. But everything seemed hopeless. The year 634 was so dreadful that afterwards the Northumbrians tried to forget it, as if it had been a nightmare too terrible ever to have happened in real life.

Irish monks in Northumbria

When it seemed that no Englishman could live in the land, a new leader appeared. Years before, a prince named Oswald had been driven from Northumbria by King Edwin. Fleeing north, to the lands of the Picts and the Scots, Oswald came at last to the island of Iona. Here there was a monastery of Irish monks, which had been founded by St Columba about sixty years before. From Iona the Scots – you may remember from page 22 that they were really the same nation as the Irish – had been taught Christianity. Oswald was not only heathen but English, too. Nevertheless, the monks of Iona received him kindly. Soon Oswald learned to love the monks and the religion they followed. He became a devout Christian.

When he heard that Edwin was dead and that his land was being destroyed by Cadwallon, Oswald came back to Northumbria. He gathered a small army around him. Near the ruins of Hadrian's Wall, on the crest of a hill, he set up his standard, a large wooden cross. He told his men that the Christian God would help them. Cadwallon, confident, attacked Oswald's little force. But Oswald had foretold truly. The Britons were swept back. Cadwallon, fleeing for his life, was caught and killed as he tried to cross a stream. His men were wiped out. To the winners, it seemed a real miracle. The Christian God had saved Northumbria after all, and Oswald was his man. The cross was left standing, and a chapel, now called St Oswald's, was built near by. The place was called Heavenfield, and bits of wood from the cross, or even moss that grew on it, were said to cure the sick.

Oswald sent back to his friends in Iona, asking for someone who would come to preach to the Northumbrians. The first monk to come was a stern man, who did not try to understand the people he was teaching. So he failed, and went back to Iona complaining that the Northumbrians were stubborn and stupid. The next monk, Aidan, was patient and kind. He had wonderful success. With Oswald as their king and Aidan as their bishop, the Northumbrians became fervent Christians. Land was given to support monasteries. Nobles and churls alike gave up their possessions and became monks. Women did the same; the most famous of these was St Hilda, who ruled as abbess over the big monastery and nunnery combined which was built at Whitby. Soon it seemed almost as though there would be more monks than warriors in the land.

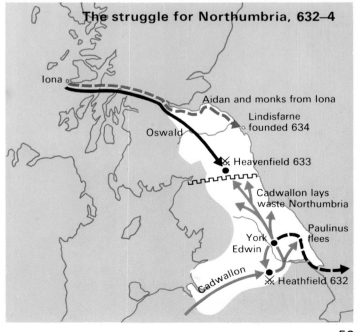

The struggle for Northumbria, 632–4

Iona

Aidan and monks from Iona

Lindisfarne founded 634

Oswald

Heavenfield 633

Cadwallon lays waste Northumbria

York
Edwin

Paulinus flees

Cadwallon

Heathfield 632

top left: Brixworth church, Northamptonshire, is practically unique, because most large Anglo-Saxon churches have been pulled down. Even this one has been altered. A row of chapels originally stood along the side of the church where the big arches are. The round stair turret at the west end was added in late Anglo-Saxon times, and the roof, battlements and upper part of the tower are relatively modern. But the body of the church is seventh century.

top right: Escomb, County Durham, is more typical in size. Except for the roof, this side is almost unchanged since the eighth century. The solid walls are made of well-cut stones looted from the ruins of a nearby Roman fort.

left: Inside Escomb church. The large windows are all later additions, and originally the little church must have been very dim. The chancel arch seems to have been taken complete from the old fort.

England is converted

For a few years Northumbria was the strongest of all the English kingdoms, as well as the most religious, and missionary monks wandered into the other kingdoms. There were disasters. Oswald himself was killed by Penda of Mercia in 641, though

The English converted from North and South

Iona

Aidan leads monks from Iona.

BERNICIA
NORTHUMBRIA

Lindisfarne
Founded by Aidan, 634.

St Cedd and three other monks sent from Lindisfarne to Mercia, 653.

DEIRA

York ●

Lincoln ●

MERCIA

Burgh Castle ● *3*
EAST ANGLIA
Dunwich ● *2*
ESSEX
Dorchester on Thames *4*
Bradwell ● *1*
WESSEX

Canterbury ●
KENT

SUSSEX

681–5.

Isle of Wight
from 686.

Felix the
Burgundian

Birinus the Roman

Converted by St Wilfrid

Celtic (British and Irish) church

1 Church of St Cedd, bishop of the East Saxons. Founded 655

3 Probable site of Celtic monastery founded by the Irish brothers Fursa and Foilan about 640

Roman church

2 Church and school of Felix the Burgundian, founded about 635.

4 Bishopric of Birinus the Roman who baptized the West Saxon king in 635.

the score was levelled when Penda was killed by the Northumbrians in 654. But while battles were lost and won, Christianity was now spreading rapidly, carried by Irish and Northumbrian monks.

At the same time, new missionaries were now reaching England from Europe, men like Felix the Burgundian who preached to the East Angles, and Birinus the Roman who preached to the West Saxons.

Spreading into England from two main directions at once, Christianity won quickly now. By about 660 the only heathen kingdom left was Sussex, small and half forgotten behind the dense forests of the Weald.

Roman or Irish?

The tonsure
marked out
a priest or monk
from ordinary men.
It also marked out Roman, left, from Celtic.

We have spent a lot of time on how Christianity came to the English. Was it really as important as all that? The answer depends on how much you think that people's beliefs are important. Christianity is still the main religion in England today, and has been since the days of Augustine and Aidan.

Now England was part of Europe again, for the English shared the same beliefs as the other peoples of Europe. But a problem remained. Would the English prefer the Roman way or the Irish?

Both Roman and Irish monks had taught the same big things, but there were noticeable small differences in the way they behaved. You already know the differences between the lives of Irish monks and those who followed the Rule of St Benedict. They looked different, too, as you can see from the pair of sketches above. The biggest difference was that they had different ways of working out the date of Easter, so that while

The organization of the Roman Church.

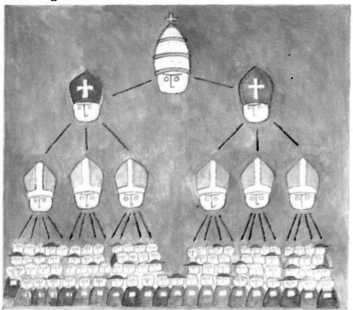

the followers of one side were celebrating the great feast, the followers of the others were still gloomily in Lent. None of these differences was really very important, but, taken together, they were a nuisance.

Much more important was this. They stood for two entirely different ways of life. Behind the Romans were the old civilized lands of the Mediterranean: there was the idea of the church organized almost as the Roman Empire had been – great, strong, disciplined and well governed, with the Pope and his bishops ruling firmly from the cities. Behind the Irish lay the misty mountains on the edge of the great ocean, the lonely monasteries and the wandering saints.

Sooner or later, the English would have to choose. It happened in 663, in Northumbria, where King Oswy was troubled by the arguments between the 'Romans', led by a young Northumbrian abbot called Wilfrid, and the 'Irish' led by Abbot Colman. He called the two leaders before him at Whitby, and heard them. Finally, Wilfrid argued that his church followed the traditions of St Peter, to whom Jesus Christ had given the keys to Heaven and Hell. (The keys are still one of the Pope's badges.) Colman could not deny it.

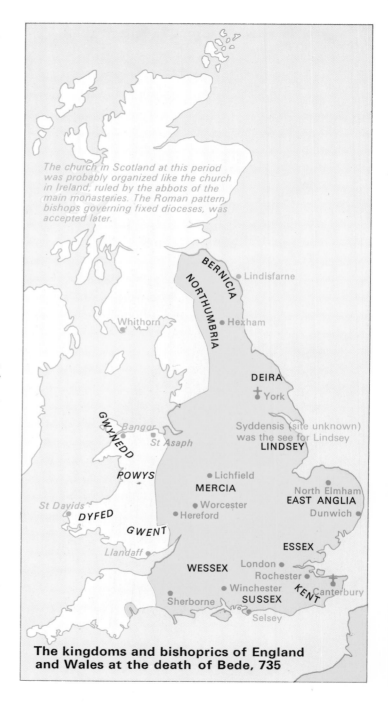

The church in Scotland at this period was probably organized like the church in Ireland, ruled by the abbots of the main monasteries. The Roman pattern, bishops governing fixed dioceses, was accepted later.

The kingdoms and bishoprics of England and Wales at the death of Bede, 735

King Oswy decided that it was safer to be on the side of St Peter.

Colman knew what his defeat meant. Northumbria had been the most 'Irish' of all the English kingdoms. It meant that the Roman church had now won all England, and Colman retired sorrowfully to the monastery of Iona.

In 668 a new archbishop was sent to Canterbury by the Pope. His name was Theodore, and he had been born in the city of Tarsus, in Asia Minor. He set about getting the church in England properly organized. The whole of England was divided into bishoprics, and the bishoprics were divided into parishes. There were two archbishops, at Canterbury and York. These two guided the bishops of southern and northern England respectively. Each bishop looked after the priests in the villages and the monks in the monasteries within his bishopric.

The English still lived in many different kingdoms, and, as you will see from the map, each bishopric lay inside its kingdom. All the same, all the English belonged to the same great church, and the authority of the archbishop of Canterbury did not stop at the frontiers of the kingdoms.

An Anglo-Saxon view of the importance of St Peter, from a book made in Winchester about 1020. The wicked enter Hell and the good wait beside the gate of Heaven while St Peter beats the Devil with his key.

left: The bishop's throne of St Wilfrid, champion of the Roman church, in the abbey which he founded at Hexham, Northumberland.

The English scholars and saints

below: The foundation stone of St Paul's church, Jarrow. The Latin inscription means: 'The dedication of the church of St Paul on 23 April in the fifteenth year of king Ecgfrith and the fourth year of Ceolfrith abbot and, under God's guidance, founder of this same church.' The year was 685.

The cross at Ruthwell, Dumfriesshire. It is of red sandstone, 15 ft (4·5 m) high. Despite its centuries in the open — it is now sheltered within the church — the carvings of Christ and the saints are still clear enough to be used to illustrate lessons and sermons, as they were in the eighth century. The photograph shows Mary Magdalen washing Christ's feet and, in the lower panel, Christ healing the blind man.

of Rome or Constantinople, these were the finest stone buildings to be made in Britain for nearly 300 years. The church at Hexham was even said to be the finest church north of the Alps. They were the beginning of English architecture.

Stone crosses, too, were set up. The elaborate decoration on them seems like Irish work. The books of these monks are more famous still. Again, the decoration resembles the Irish style. Compare the ornamental page overleaf with that on page 48 of this book. It seems likely that Irish and Northumbrian artists learned from each other, and between them produced books which are now among the most treasured possessions of the English and Irish nations.

Some of these monks were famous for studying and writing, not merely decorating books. The libraries and schools of Northumbria were respected all over Christian Europe, and St Bede, of Wearmouth-Jarrow, was the best scholar of his time. Most of his books were about the Scriptures, of course, but nowadays that which is most often read is his book about how the English became Christians; it is the very first English history book. The quotations on pages 50 and 52 of this book are taken from it. Bede died in 735.

The Lindisfarne Gospels,
one of the most splendidly
decorated books in the world,
was made about 710.
This page is the beginning of
the Gospel of St Mark.

Half a century later, when the great King Charles of the Franks, master of western Europe, wanted to improve the education of his people, he sent to Northumbria. From the fine school at York came the learned Alcuin, to bring better learning to the Franks.

Missionaries, too, came from Northumbria. St. Wilfrid, whom you met at Whitby, converted the last of the English heathen in Sussex, and began to preach to the Frisians. Willibrord of Ripon carried on the conversion of the Frisians.

The greatest of all the English missionaries was not a Northumbrian, but a West Saxon. He took the Latin name of Boniface and, going to the help of Willibrord, converted many of the tribesmen who dwelt in the forests of Germany. In 754 he was murdered by some of the heathen, but his work had been well done. It has been said of him: 'No Englishman has ever played so great a part in central Europe.'

You can compare this map with that on page 49. Once again a nation living in Britain had first received Christianity; then, about a century later, repaid the debt by sending out missionaries and scholars. Britain had been given much, and now in her turn she was giving.

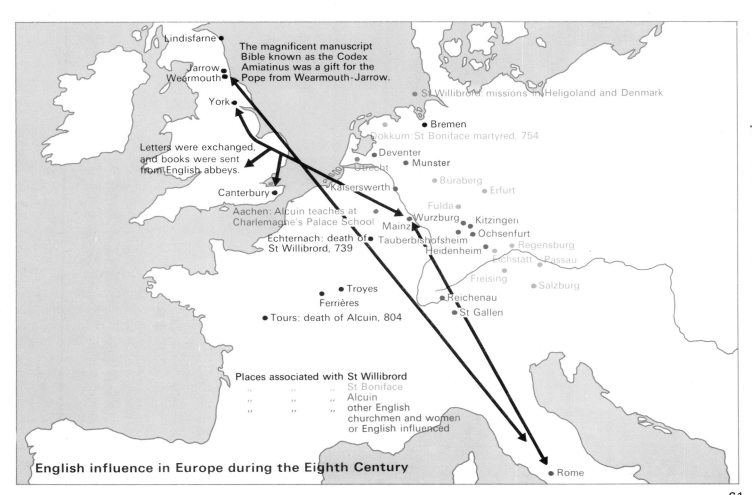

English influence in Europe during the Eighth Century

A leaf from an ivory diptych, carved about 355. It is believed to show a rich family watching the races in the Hippodrome of Constantinople. It is about 11·5 in. (280 mm)

Byzantium: the Rome of the East

The city of Istanbul is still often called Constantinople, and was also called Byzantium. It was the capital of the Eastern Roman Empire, which is usually known as the Byzantine Empire. Here, while the barbarians in the west were slowly setting up their kingdoms and learning Christianity, a splendid civilization still carried on the proud traditions of the past without a break.

The pictures on these pages will show you some of the most remarkable things about Byzantine life. Like the Romans, these people loved the excitement of the chariot races; the Blue and Green teams were supported passionately, and even became the symbols of political parties. Unlike the Romans, though, the Byzantines did not care for the gladiatorial butcheries of the arena; perhaps because they had many Greek ideas, or perhaps because they were Christians.

Opposite you see the great church of the Holy Wisdom, still one of the most marvellous buildings in the world. On the next page you see the sort of pictures of Christ and His saints – icons, as they are called – before which the Byzantines prayed. Painted on the walls or made of mosaic, they had something stiff, dignified and mysterious about them. If you can imagine one *right:* The Church of the Holy Wisdom, Hagia Sophia. The minarets and some of the lower extensions were added by the Turks after they took the city in 1453 and turned the church into a mosque; but the main building, with its magnificently engineered central dome and supporting half-domes, is the work of Byzantine architects of the 530s.

below: The Golden Horn, the long bay which forms the harbour of Constantinople. In times of danger it could be closed, and became part of the defences.

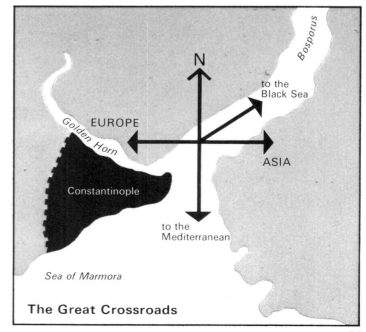

The Great Crossroads

of the great Byzantine churches with the rich colours and the staring eyes of the icons glowing in the lamplight through the incense-smoke, you can guess that this seemed hardly to belong to the world of human beings. These people were tremendously concerned about their religion, and it sometimes happened that an emperor would persecute some of his people because he did not think that they understood Christianity correctly.

The picture on the right shows one of the most famous Byzantine emperors, Justinian, who reigned from 527 to 565. He did many great works; he built the church you have just seen. But he is best remembered for his Code of Laws. You know what fine law-makers the Romans had been. As time went on, though, laws had been made and changed and added together until there was such a vast collection that nobody, not even the judges, could use them properly. So Justinian gave orders that they should be sorted out and written down as briefly as possible. His helpers had to examine over 1,600 books containing 3,000,000 lines. In three years they reduced all this to 150,000 lines. It was a job worthy of the old Romans at their best.

Were the Byzantines really Romans? They called themselves Romans, and Justinian's laws were mostly written down in Latin. But you have seen that there was a difference. By the end of his reign Justinian was usually writing in Greek, and this was the language used by most Byzantines. It had been the main language of the Middle East since the time of Alexander, and even the Romans had not changed this.

left: This icon was made in the sixth century. It was not painted, but made from dyed waxes applied with a heated rod. It measures 20·5 × 15 in. (520 × 390 mm) and is in the remote monastery of St Catherine on Mount Sinai, where monks of the Orthodox church continue to work and pray.

right: The Emperor Justinian and some of his court, portrayed in a large mosaic on the wall of the church of St Vitale, Ravenna, which was built in his reign.

MAXIMIANVS

65

The Romans had been famous as soldiers and engineers. The Greeks were better known for cleverness. If you look at the next map, and see all the dangers to the Eastern Empire; and then think that it lasted for a thousand years after the Western Empire; then you may guess that the Byzantines had some of the qualities of both Romans and Greeks.

The heart of the Empire, Byzantium itself, was protected by its mighty three-fold walls. From this strategic stronghold, placed where Europe meets Asia and land meets sea, the emperor held his own against all his different enemies. The symbols on the map will show you how.

First, he used money. He sent to kings and chiefs beyond his frontiers splendidly clothed ambassadors, carrying splendid presents. When a barbarian chief came to visit Byzantium, the splendour was such as to amaze him with the wealth and power of the emperor. To his friends, the emperor gave rich gifts. It was good to be his friend.

Buying friendship like this could have been very dangerous. Why should not the barbarians attack Byzantium and take all its treasures for themselves? There would have been a very serious danger if Byzantium had been weak; but Byzantium had an excellent army and navy.

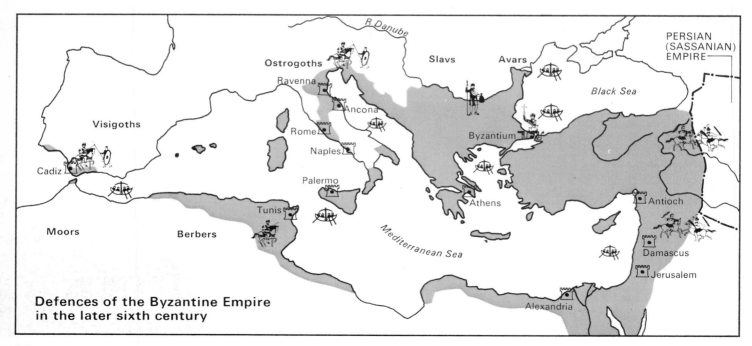

Defences of the Byzantine Empire in the later sixth century

Part of the triple wall built to protect
Constantinople by the Emperor Theodosius II
in the early fifth century. The diagram to the
right shows a section through the walls when
they were in use.

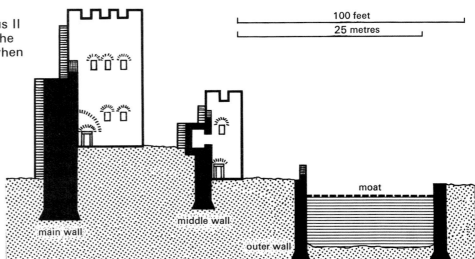

100 feet

25 metres

main wall

middle wall

outer wall

moat

An outpost of the Byzantine Empire: Ain Tounga, Tunisia. It was linked to faraway Byzantium by the imperial navy. Its projecting towers, from which archers could sweep the walls, seem small-scale copies of those on the walls of the great city.

All around the Empire lay walled cities, or forts like this one. From these bases the army could operate against invaders. It was a real army, not a horde of warriors. The soldiers were professionals, very skilled. They used maps, had engineers, practised all sorts of tactics. The generals studied books about the art of war, and sometimes wrote such books themselves. The most important regiments were heavy cavalry; they had armour, lance and sword for charging, but were also armed with powerful short bows like those of nomad horsemen. An army like this could fight anywhere against any foe.

The map on page 66 also shows you how the Byzantine Empire lies around seas. These seas were ruled by the Byzantine navy. It was not only that the ships and sailors were good; they also had a secret weapon. This was 'Greek Fire'. Its secret was so well kept that we do not know quite how it was made, but it could be pumped out of metal tubes or thrown in earthenware pots. It would set anything ablaze and could not be extinguished by water. The navy made it easy for the army to move from one place to another, as one enemy after another seemed dangerous.

Behind this shield, the people of the Eastern Empire could go on with the industry and trade that made them rich. The big cities – Alexandria, Damascus, Antioch – were prosperous. The wealth went in taxes to the emperor, and you have seen how he used it.

In the early seventh century, despite some misfortunes, the Byzantine Empire seemed especially successful and strong. The barbarians north of the Balkans and the Black Sea, Slavs and nomads alike, had been held back. In the west, the emperor's armies had beaten the Goths in Italy and the Vandals in North Africa, and were taking back the lost provinces of the old Western Roman Empire. In the east, most important of all, they had inflicted a crushing defeat upon the only civilized enemy, the Sassanian Persian Empire, in 638. Just about the time Christianity was reaching the remote villages of the English barbarians, the Byzantines seemed to be spreading wider their great civilized Empire.

Even to the south, up the valley of the Nile, Byzantium had spread its influence, in art and in religion, to the kingdoms of Nubia and Ethiopia. But the southern borders of the Byzantine Empire were mostly deserts, crossed by caravans of traders and inhabited by poverty-stricken nomads. To the south, it seemed, there were neither opportunities nor dangers.

Greek Fire in action. Though this drawing was not made until about 700 years after Greek fire was first used, we have no other Byzantine picture of their famous flame-throwers.

Muhammad, Prophet of Allah

Arabia stretches for about a million and a quarter square miles. There are a few reasonably fertile places; once, in the south, there had been small but rich kingdoms, like Sheba, depending mostly on irrigation. Most of the land, though, was desert or poor steppe. The people lived on their flocks or by trading in caravans, but it was difficult to earn a good living.

No one king ruled over all the Arabs. Each town and each wandering tribe did as it thought fit. It was the same with religion. Most Arabs worshipped many gods, and spirits which were believed to dwell in rocks and trees. They sometimes made statues of their gods, and they worshipped and made sacrifices to these and to stones which were especially sacred. In the town of Mecca there was a temple, the Kaaba, in which there were idols and a very holy black stone. Arabs came on pilgrimage to touch the stone and gain holiness from it.

There were other religions in Arabia. After the Jews had been driven out of Palestine by the Romans, a number of them had settled in Arabia. From them some of the Arabs learned to believe that there was only one God. Christians, too, came with the merchant caravans. Christianity was by now the religion of Ethiopia, and for a few years in the middle of the sixth century the Ethiopians held part of South Arabia.

This was Arabia about 570, when Muhammad was born in the holy city of Mecca. He was born into a powerful tribe, but was an orphan from the age of six. He knew what it was to be poor. He earned his living in the camel caravans. One of the people who employed him was a rich widow, who came to admire him greatly. They were married, and Muhammad became a wealthy merchant. We know very little more than this about his life before he was about forty years old, but it seems that he used to go into the desert sometimes, to think and pray undisturbed. While he was doing this he saw a vision of the angel Gabriel. The angel began to teach him many things, and ordered him to pass these teachings to all.

At first Muhammad wondered if he was dreaming, or perhaps going mad. But he talked to his wife and his closest friends, and they believed in him and his visions. So he began to teach as the angel had ordered.

His teachings were more like those of the Jews and Christians than those of the other Arabs. He said that there was one Allah, which is simply the Arabic word for God. Allah wished men to be good. He would reward good men who believed in him; anyone killed for Allah's sake would go straight to Paradise. Allah was all-knowing and all-powerful; long ago he had decided all that would happen, and the fate of every man. From those whom he had decided to reward, Allah insisted on complete loyalty.

'There is no god but Allah,
and Muhammad is His Prophet.'

The leaders of new religions are often unpopular, especially if they talk like that in the holy city of the old gods. Muhammad said that Allah wished all idols to be destroyed, for it was blasphemous to make various pictures and statues, especially of false gods. The men of Mecca jeered at him and insulted him. His followers, especially if they were poor men or slaves, were beaten and tortured, and only the protection of his uncle, who was a man of great influence, saved Muhammad himself. His own tribe were his worst enemies. At last, after both his wife and his uncle had died, the Prophet decided to flee.

This was the Hijra, or Flight, and Muhammadans count

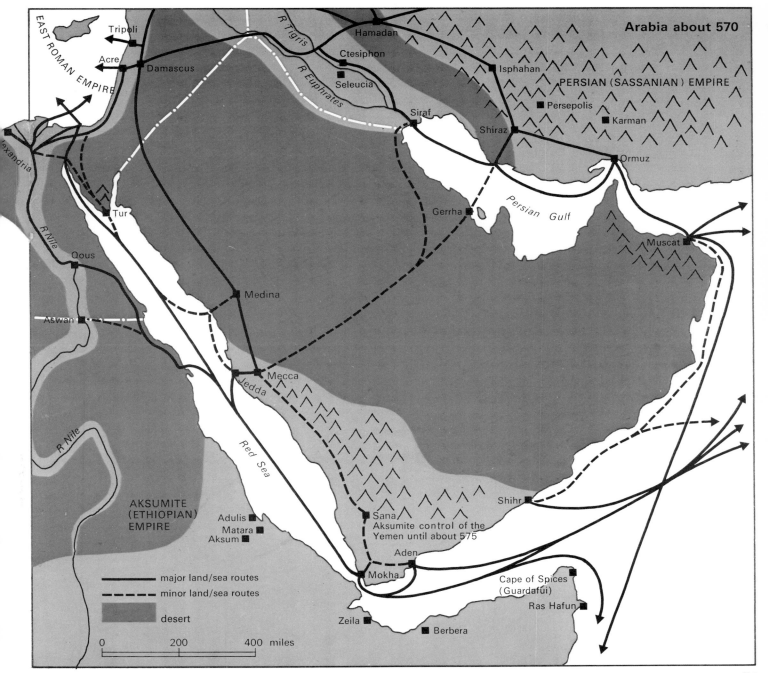

Arabia about 570

EAST ROMAN EMPIRE

Tripoli
Acre
Damascus
Alexandria
R Nile
Tur
Qous
Aswan
R Nile

R Tigris
R Euphrates
Hamadan
Ctesiphon
Seleucia
Isphahan
PERSIAN (SASSANIAN) EMPIRE
Persepolis
Karman
Shiraz
Siraf
Ormuz
Gerrha
Persian Gulf
Muscat

Medina
Mecca
Jedda
Red Sea
Shihr

AKSUMITE (ETHIOPIAN) EMPIRE
Adulis
Matara
Aksum
Sana
Aksumite control of the Yemen until about 575
Aden
Mokha
Cape of Spices (Guardafui)
Ras Hafun
Zeila
Berbera

major land/sea routes
minor land/sea routes
desert

0   200   400 miles

years from it just as Christians count from the birth of Christ. The Hijra happened in A.D. 622 of the Christian way of reckoning. Muhammad had been invited to go to Medina, where many men believed in what he said, and here he fled, 300 miles across the desert from Mecca.

It was the turning point. Muhammad was soon the master of Medina, and the Muslims, as his followers were called, began to attack the caravans of Mecca. In the battles which followed the Muslims usually did well, and even when they lost they believed that their dead had gone to Paradise. By argument and by the sword, the Prophet spread Islam, as the religion of Allah was called. Though he was a kind and merciful man usually, Muhammad could be harsh to any whom he thought obstinately wicked; men might be beheaded, women and children enslaved, according to the old custom. But generally he stopped fierce old habits of feuding and killing.

By 630 Muhammad was so strong that he was able to enter Mecca without a fight. He destroyed the idols of the Kaaba and made it a holy place for all Muslims. All over Arabia men turned to Islam. In every town, five times a day, the muezzin called 'Allah is greatest! Allah is greatest! There is no god but

above: The mosque at Samarra, built in the ninth century, is the largest in Islam. This view shows the outer wall with its semicircular towers, and an unusually shaped minaret.
right: The Dome of the Rock, Jerusalem, was built in the seventh century to a design which shows that the architects admired Byzantine churches. Jerusalem, already a holy city to Jews and Christians, now became a holy city to Muslims also, for it was from this rock that Muhammad was said to have risen to Heaven.

Allah! Muhammad is the Prophet of Allah! Come to prayer!' And the Faithful turned in the direction of Mecca, and prayed. The Bedouins, too, the nomads of the desert, also prayed, spreading out their mats beneath them so that they should be sure of worshipping Allah in a clean place.

Muhammad wrote no books, but his followers wrote down many of his words. When he said such things as 'Allah loves those who judge fairly' or 'Your slaves are your brethren', they were remembered, and later collected into a book which is called the Koran, and is to the Muslims what the Bible is to Christians.

The conquests of the Arabs

When Muhammad died in 632, Islam was the faith of almost all the Arabs. Yet this religion was meant for all mankind, and already the Prophet had sent letters to the rulers of Ethiopia, of Persia and of Byzantium, calling on them to accept Islam. Now the Muslims were ready to carry Islam far and wide upon the points of their spears.

Look carefully at the next map. Notice the extent of the lands which the Arabs conquered, and notice the dates. Within a few years they had destroyed the Persian Empire, which had already been weakened by the Byzantines, and set up their capital in the ancient home of civilization, on the banks of the Tigris. They had shattered Byzantine armies and conquered some of the richest parts of the Eastern Empire, Syria and Palestine and Egypt, with their rich and crowded cities. Here their victory was made easier because the people of those lands were tired of the heavy taxes of the emperor, and had known persecution because some of them thought differently from the emperor about some points in the Christian religion; they expected better treatment from the Muslims, and they were right. In North Africa the fierce Berbers became Muslims themselves, and added new strength to the Arab armies. In Spain the Visigothic kings and nobles had never won the loyalty of the people as a whole, and so, when they were beaten in battle, that was the end of them.

So the Arab conquests swept on for a century. The whole

It is very difficult to discover what the warriors of Islam looked like at the time of the great conquests, but this bowl may give some clues. It was made in Mesopotamia during the tenth century, is of yellow lustre and measures 9·5 in. (241 mm) across.

of Christian Europe might have fallen before them. In 717 they launched a tremendous attack on the city of Byzantium itself. The struggle raged for a whole year, but the triple walls held. The Arabs fell back. In 732, at the other end of Christendom, a Muslim army drove deep into the land of the Franks. Near Tours it was smashed by the mail-clad horsemen of the Frankish leader, Charles the Hammer. These were the limits of the astonishing Arab victories.

It may sound, from what you have just read, that the Arabs did best against kingdoms which had serious weaknesses; this is true, and it is only common-sense, anyway. But this does not mean that Arab warriors were anything but excellent fighters. You would expect them to be. They were tough men of the desert, with everything to gain and nothing to lose. Now they were held together by one religion, and obeyed one leader – the Caliph, the Commander of the Faithful, the successor of the Prophet. They knew that if they were killed in this holy war, Allah would reward them generously in Paradise. And they believed that Allah, the all-powerful, had decided from the beginning that Islam should triumph: it was written, it was Fate. Strengthened thus, they swept on to found a great Empire and a noble civilization.

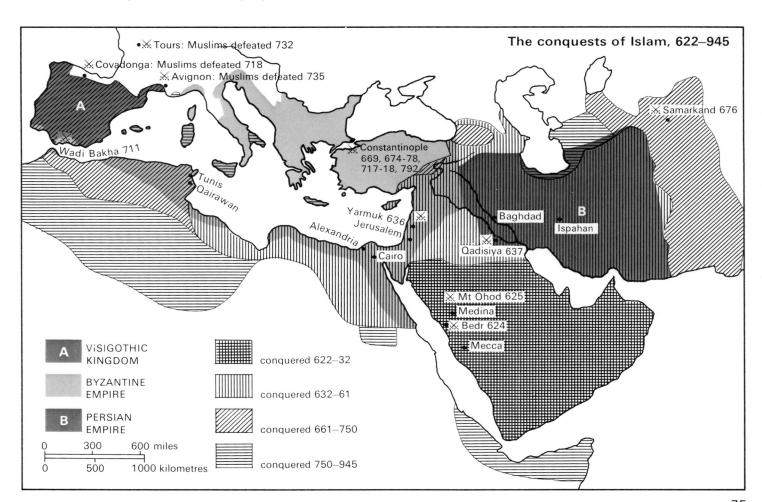

The conquests of Islam, 622–945

Tours: Muslims defeated 732
Covadonga: Muslims defeated 718
Avignon: Muslims defeated 735
Samarkand 676
A
Wadi Bakha 711
Constantinople 669, 674-78, 717-18, 792
Tunis
Qairawan
Baghdad
B
Ispahan
Yarmuk 636
Jerusalem
Alexandria
Qadisiya 637
Cairo
Mt Ohod 625
Medina
Bedr 624
Mecca

A   VISIGOTHIC KINGDOM
conquered 622–32

BYZANTINE EMPIRE
conquered 632–61

B   PERSIAN EMPIRE
conquered 661–750

0   300   600 miles
0   500   1000 kilometres
conquered 750–945

The civilization of Islam

There was some destruction when the conquering Muslims became masters of the ancient civilized lands. Usually, though, the Muslims respected what they found: cities full of merchants trading with distant lands and craftsmen skilled in metal and wood and leather; hot, dry lands made fertile by irrigation. The Arabs kept these things going, and they built splendidly themselves.

The fabulous city of the Caliphs, Baghdad, was wrecked by later conquerors after six brilliant centuries, so that we cannot now have much idea of its former splendours. In other towns we can still see some of the best Muslim, or Islamic buildings; often they are mosques, like the ones on the following pages. With their graceful domes and minarets, their forests of delicate pillars and arches, these show a new and beautiful style of architecture which Muslims went on using for many centuries to come.

You may remember that Muhammad disapproved of several types of pictures or statues. That meant that if the Muslims wanted to decorate anything – and they were fond of ornament – they had to invent patterns and designs. Here are some of them. You may be reminded sometimes of beasts or flowers, and you may be interested to compare them with the Irish and Northumbrian work which you saw on pages 48 and 60.

A ninth-century bowl from Samarkand, 4·5 in. (114·3 mm) across and 0·5 in. (12·7 mm) high. The black decoration on the white earthenware is in fact an inscription in Kufic, one of the forms of writing developed in the Muslim world. It reads: 'Blessing and ease to the owner'.

Eighth-century mosaics in the great mosque of Damascus.

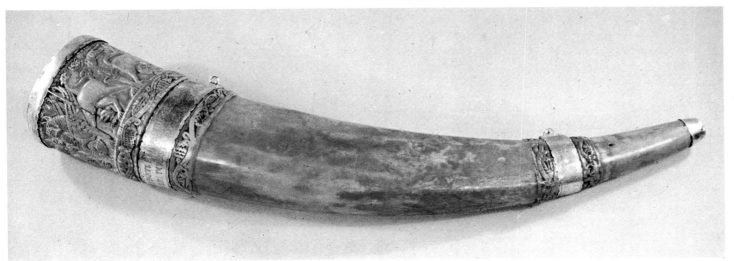

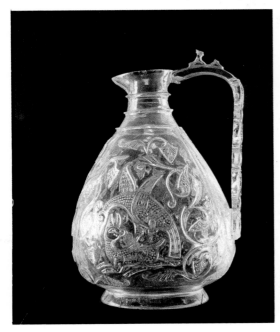

below: Rock crystal jug made in late tenth-century Egypt, possibly for the Caliph. Height 8.5 in (216 mm), diameter of the base 5.5 in. (140 mm).

below: Eighth- or ninth-century silk fabric with stylized animals, probably woven in or near Samarkand.

above: The Horn of Ulf, kept in York Minster since *c.* 1025, is a 2.5 ft (762 mm) ivory tusk carved in what seems to be Sicilian Muslim style.

Some of the decoration you have just been looking at is simply writing, used as ornament. It is Arabic writing, very different from the letters which are used in this book. The Arabic language spread all over the lands conquered by the Muslims, as you may remember from the map on page 5. But not all the people who spoke and wrote Arabic were either Arabs or Muslims. These conquerors turned out to be quite tolerant. Many of them saw no reason for trying to force such people as Jews or Christians to become Muslims. Perhaps it was better to leave Allah to open the eyes of such unbelievers when he willed. Meanwhile, provided they paid extra taxes, they could live peacefully under the Muslims. In this way many learned Jews and Christians wrote and taught in Arabic, beside Muslim scholars.

They collected and translated many books of the Greek and Roman philosophers and scientists, besides writing new ones. Though they wrote history and geography books, not to mention stories for sheer amusement which everybody still knows (even if only from pantomimes or children's story books),

The main entrance to the citadel of Aleppo, built in the twelfth century. It displays not only massive strength, but also skill in the designing of positions from which the defenders could shoot.

above: Inside the eighth-century mosque — now a cathedral — at Cordoba. The rows of double arches poised over a forest of slender pillars could possibly have been inspired by Roman aqueducts, but, even if this is true, only a brilliant architect would have thought of using the idea in such an original fashion.

top right: The mosque of Ibn Tulun, Cairo, built a few years after Samarra and to a similar plan. This photograph shows the interior of the court; the small building in the centre contains a fountain where the worshippers may clean themselves before praying.

right: A reminder of where Islam began. The simple shrine of a Muslin saint in the lonely desert of Southern Arabia.

the Arabic scholars were best of all in science. There were skilled botanists and chemists and doctors. Many were students of astronomy. As for their interest in mathematics, you need only remember that the numerals we all use today are called Arabic (though the Arabs may have borrowed them from India; we cannot be sure) and that Algebra is an Arabic expression (it means 'the putting together of broken parts').

Within their cities the Arabs built palaces and mosques, colleges and libraries. There were fine hospitals in some cities, with their own specialists, dispensaries and libraries. There were many public baths; 900, it is said, in Cordoba alone. There were fine city walls and bridges. Men who could afford it made gardens with rare plants and fountains. Poets were popular and well rewarded, and chess was a favourite game.

Though there were quarrels among the rulers, and the great empire of the Caliph was soon split, the Muslims kept their unity of language and culture. From their cities, they could look with equal scorn upon the rude and primitive savages, the black ones to the south and the white ones to the north.

Charles the Great and his new Roman Empire

This is as near as we can get to a portrait of Charles the Great. It is a statuette, about 9·5 in. (240 mm) high, cast in 869. The horse is a later replacement.

In 768 a young man of about twenty-six became king of the Franks. His name was Charles. He was grandson of that Charles the Hammer who had stopped the Muslims at Tours, and was to become greater still.

He was tall and strong, with fair hair and a long moustache, and he always wore his sword. He was interested in everything, and never tired. He could read Latin, and understood some Greek, as well as his own language. He had books read to him at meal-times. When he was old, he tried to learn to write himself. Always he was on the move, fighting his enemies or inspecting the way his lands were being ruled by his servants. He was enormously strong and energetic; he had to be.

When Charles came to the throne, the kingdom of the Franks was powerful, but it was not surrounded by friends. The first map will show you the position. To the east were Germanic tribes, many of them still heathen; south, the Muslims of Spain. In Italy things were very confused, with the Pope trying to keep himself and the country around Rome free from the Byzantines and the fierce Lombards, who had settled in the plain of northern Italy. Among kings, warfare was their normal way of passing the time. But of all these experienced fighters, Charles became the greatest.

As you may guess, his success was sometimes bought dearly. The most famous story which has come down to us from his wars is of the last stand of two of his bravest warriors, Roland and Oliver. They and their men died like heroes in the Pass of Roncesvalles; but it was not a victory. That was on the Spanish frontier. On the opposite side of his kingdom, the Saxons (not the people who lived in England, but those whose ancestors had remained in Germany) were not finally forced to accept Charles as their king and Christianity as their religion for twenty-five years; and then only after such ferocious punishments as the massacre in 782, when Charles had 4,500 Saxon rebels beheaded at one time. The picture which seems most to sum up the mighty king of the Franks, however, is this, written by someone who lived shortly afterwards: 'The Iron King, crowned with his Iron Helm, with sleeves of iron mail on his arms, his broad breast protected by an iron byrnie, and an iron lance in his left hand, his right free to grasp his unconquered sword.'

The next map shows you what Charles did. He brought under his rule all the Germanic nations on the mainland of Europe; and around this Empire, guarding against attacks from such

The Frankish Empire and neighbouring peoples at the accession of Charles the Great, 768

peoples as the Slavs and the Avars, many of whom had already learnt to dread his 'unconquered sword', he set up frontier districts called Marks, or Marches.

In the year 800, Charles was spending Christmas in Rome. The Pope was now free from both the Byzantines and the Lombards; instead, he was under the protection of Charles. On Christmas Day, when Charles went to Mass in the church of St Peter, the Pope placed on his head a crown, and hailed him as Roman emperor.

It may or may not have been a surprise to Charles. It was certainly a shock in Byzantium, where the eastern emperor still claimed to be rightfully the ruler of all the old Roman Empire, Western as well as Eastern. But Charles was too strong to be challenged. And as he was so religious, had been crowned by the Pope, and thought that one of the most important duties of any ruler was to serve God and defend the church, this new Roman Empire became known as the Holy Roman Empire.

Ruling this Empire was an even greater task than building it. You saw on page 17 how, when the barbarians took over, the old civilized habits had gradually fallen away. Charles had to rule an empire where the fine roads and rich cities, the trade and industry were in decay. Instead of educated governors,

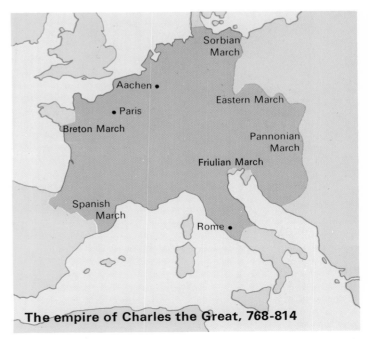

The empire of Charles the Great, 768-814

judges and civil servants, he had to rely on warrior-nobles to serve him. By now there were few well-educated men in the whole of Christian Europe, except for priests and monks; hardly anyone else could even read and write.

Charles did his best with the men he had. He put his most trusted warriors in charge of districts. These counts, as they were called, had to keep law and order in their districts, or counties; and they had to raise warriors and bring them to join the emperor whenever there was a war – which was often. The counts were very powerful in their counties. Could they always be trusted to use their power well?

There were two ways of checking on them. One was for Charles to send special envoys from his court, to look at various districts and bring back reports. The other way was to go and see for himself. He had a number of palaces rather like the one shown in the picture, but he did not often stay for long in any one of them. With his advisers and envoys, servants, clerks and escort, he moved from place to place. The court, all those people and the animals and furnishings, never seemed settled. It had the extra advantage that these moves made it easier to feed the court; they could eat the food stored up in

one place and then move on, so that there was not much of a problem of transporting food. Also, each palace could be given a good 'spring clean' while it was empty; this was very much needed after it had been crowded for a week or two, for cleanliness and sanitation had been among the things which had fallen off when the barbarians came.

What Charles needed were educated men. You saw on page 61 how he sent for Alcuin of York. Throughout his Empire he encouraged the study and copying of books. Many of them, and many of his government papers, were written in a new form of writing which we could easily read today. Charles did not want education to be something for priests and monks only. At his palace school his own family and the children of

The palace at Aachen where Charles the Great spent most of his time when he was old. The main buildings, with their rounded arches, are in the tradition of Roman and Byzantine architecture, while the thatch and timber outer buildings are in the barbarian tradition. This model has been photographed on a street plan of modern Aachen, where the church still stands.

his counts and other nobles were taught. So Charles tried to look after the future rulers of his Holy Roman Empire.

But could such an Empire have a future? Could it be held together by anyone but the giant who had made it? Charles himself seems to have had his doubts, because in 806 he made a will dividing his lands between his three sons; each was to be a king, and Charles did not say which of them was to have the title of Emperor. He never had to decide, for two of his sons died. So in 813 Charles placed the Imperial Crown on the head of his one remaining son. In 814 the old emperor died. He is known as Charlemagne, or Charles the Great.

The new emperor is known as Louis the Pious. As the name suggests, he was a good man. But there is a difference between being a good man and being a good emperor. Louis was not strong enough for the job. His own sons fought against him and among themselves. He was still emperor when he died in 840. Three years later his sons did as the map below shows.

Lothar, the eldest, was emperor. His share had to include both Aachen, the main palace of Charles the Great, and Rome. It was called Lotharingia.

Charles the Bald took the western third, where the people spoke a language which had once been Latin, and was now an early form of French.

Louis the German took the eastern third. His people mostly belonged to the tribes conquered by Charles the Great.

The kingdom of Charles lived, and grew into modern France. The kingdom of Louis likewise grew into modern Germany. Lotharingia lasted until 870, when the other two shared it between them; today its only trace on the map of Europe is the region in France called Lorraine.

Nowadays both the French and the Germans think of Charles the Great as one of their own national heroes, and both are right. His work led to the birth of those two great nations. His idea of a new Roman Empire turned out to be only a dream. But it was a mighty dream, a dream that other men after him were to go on dreaming for hundreds of years.

The beginning of the Book of Exodus from Alcuin's Bible. This manuscript was copied by Benedictine monks at Tours in France, *c.* 825–50.

The treaty of Verdun, 843

The Northmen

'From the fury of the Northmen, good Lord deliver us.' That was the prayer offered up in countless Christian churches, year after year, during the two centuries after the death of Charles the Great.

The Northmen were the last of the Germanic barbarians to attack western Europe, and in some ways they were the most dangerous. This map shows their home-lands. It is really a continuation northward of the map on page 13. These people lived, like the other barbarians, in their wooden settlements among the forests and hills, valleys and plains of Scandinavia. The Goths and some of the invaders of Britain may have come originally from parts of Scandinavia, but on the whole the northern peoples do not seem to have been very important in the big invasions of barbarian tribes which broke up the Roman Empire. Why, then, did they burst out now?

They were not being pushed by any other people, but it may be that they were pushing themselves. Those northern countries are not very fertile, and it seems as though the population was growing too fast for everybody to have a good living. Besides, there were quarrels; some men wished to get away from chiefs or kings whom they disliked. For reasons like these, people have migrated all through history – you may remember the Greek colonies 1,500 years earlier. But the Northmen were not simply colonists. Sometimes, it is true, they settled in lands across the seas. What has made them famous, however, is that many of them became Vikings, or sea-rovers.

These men were ready to make a good living for themselves in any way which seemed convenient: trade, robbery, slaving, blackmail, fighting for pay, it was all one to them. The life of a Viking was hard and often short, but it was exciting; to a barbarian, it seemed a real man's life. After the earlier Viking raids proved successful, more and more of the men of Norway, Sweden and Denmark took to this way of life.

Probably most people today think of the Vikings as fine sailors and fierce warriors. Truly, they were both. But often people imagine the typical Viking to be a half-mad savage lusting for blood, winning through sheer brute strength without much brain-power. Such a picture is not true. Though there were a few, the Berserkers, who used to work themselves crazy in battle and lay about them with the strength of madmen, most Vikings seem to have been shrewd and skilful, as well as brave. You can see this from their ships, their arms, and the way they planned their expeditions.

We know a lot about the Viking warships, because some of them have been found lying under mounds where they were buried with the chiefs who had owned them. Whole books have been written about them, explaining how wonderfully designed and made they were. These pictures may help you to understand the thought and skill and hard work of the men who built them. See the shape of the hull, with the narrow prow to cut the water and the broad middle to ride over the waves. The planks were tied instead of nailed to the ribs, so that the ship would 'give' a little and so stand up to wind and sea more easily. Notice also the carefully balanced steering oar. In 1893 a replica of one of these ships was sailed from Norway to America in four weeks. Here are some of the captain's remarks: 'All this elasticity, combined with the fine lines, naturally made for speed . . . The rudder is nothing short of brilliant.'

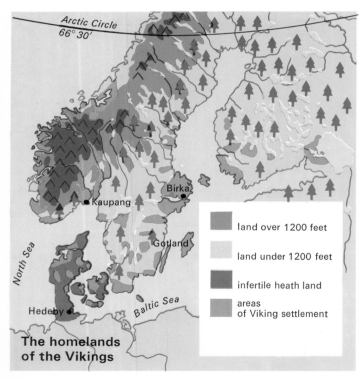

Arctic Circle
66° 30'

Birka

Kaupang

Gotland

North Sea

Hedeby

Baltic Sea

land over 1200 feet

land under 1200 feet

infertile heath land

areas of Viking settlement

The homelands of the Vikings

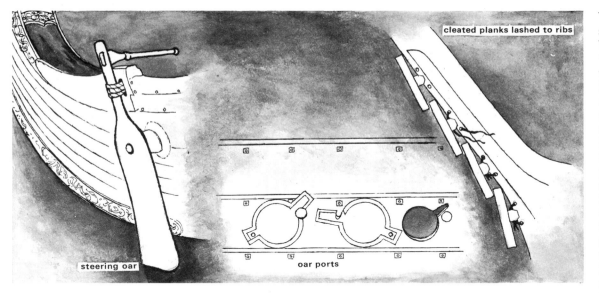

cleated planks lashed to ribs

steering oar

oar ports

These drawings show details of Viking ship design:
1. The 'steer board' was pivoted on a large wooden knob, carefully balanced so that it could easily be controlled by the tiller. The lashing near the top prevented it from swinging wildly.
2. The oar ports were exactly shaped for the oars to be slid through, with covers on the inside.
3. The cleats were not fixed to the planks, but were part of them, carved from the same piece of solid oak. This sectional diagram shows how the planks were tied so as to overlap. Where they overlapped they were riveted tightly together.

In 1935 a Danish warship was found in a tenth-century burial at Ladby, on the island of Fünen. It measured 72 ft (22 m) by 10 ft (3 m). A full-scale replica was made, and this photograph shows an experiment to discover how — or if — horses could be transported on such vessels.

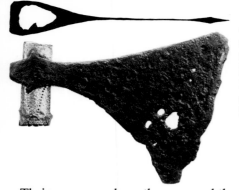

An eleventh-century axe-head found in the Thames at London. The overall width is 9·5 in. (241·5 mm).

Their weapons show the same subtle skill. You may think that a great battle-axe, like this, is obviously the weapon of a brute; but see how the position and shape of the edge has been thought out. And look at the view from above, which shows you how the blade has been made far lighter than you would expect at first glance. The horned and winged helmets, by the way, probably belong only to the story-books. The evidence suggests that Vikings wore plain, smooth helmets. Anyway, they would have had far too much sense to wear such clumsy ornaments in battle.

They showed the same intelligence on their raids. A small raid would strike quickly at some exposed but rich target, for example, the monastery on the island of Lindisfarne. The raiders would be away before help could reach their victims, darting away to another place. Over a distance, the ships could move much faster than an army marching along the coast.

A big raid, when there were ships enough to make a fleet and men to make an army, would work differently. The sketches show you how. The fleet would sail to a place where the ships could be safely beached or moored; it could be on the coast, but could be far inland, on a river. Then a ditch and rampart would be dug, so that the Vikings had a fortified base. While some remained on guard, the others would steal all the horses they could, and set out to plunder far and wide. If these men should meet the men of the local count, or even the king, they would dismount and fight. Since the Vikings were often experienced warriors, while many of the men in the defending armies would be peasants who had spent their lives using spade and scythe rather than spear and sword, the Vikings had a very good chance of winning. Even if they lost, they had their base and their ships behind them.

How to conduct a successful Viking raid

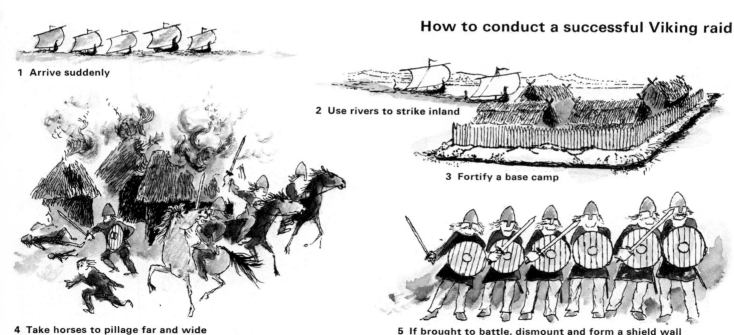

1 Arrive suddenly

2 Use rivers to strike inland

3 Fortify a base camp

4 Take horses to pillage far and wide

5 If brought to battle, dismount and form a shield wall

In small pirate bands or in big armies, as traders or robbers or settlers, the Northmen spread in all directions. The map shows where they went and what they did. Pushing along the east European rivers, they set up towns among the Slavs; from these small beginnings the great Russian Empire was to grow hundreds of years later. Some went further, trading and fighting with the Muslims and the Byzantines, or joining the emperor's guard in Byzantium – they gave that much-named city yet one more name, Micklegarth. Over the western seas Norse settlers went to Iceland, where their descendants still live, and from here they founded settlements in Greenland and even, for a few years, in America. Further south, you can see how the Northmen settled on islands and round coasts; this was usually when the people already living there were rather weak, but one group, led by Rolf the Ganger, were able to make even the Frankish king give them land, Normandy, as it was called after them. In time, many of them did good to the places where they settled; but in the ninth and tenth centuries it was their bad side which most other people saw.

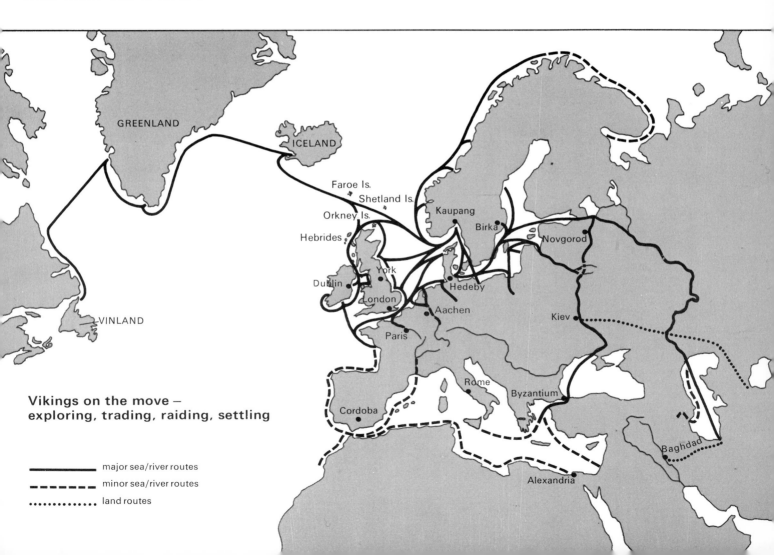

**Vikings on the move –
exploring, trading, raiding, settling**

——————— major sea/river routes

– – – – – minor sea/river routes

················· land routes

The defence of the West

During the years when the Vikings were ravaging from the seas, western Europe was attacked by a new wave of nomads from the eastern steppes. These were the Magyars, or Hungarians; they had a great deal in common with the earlier Huns. They made their camps on the broad pastures by the Danube, and from here raided deep into the more settled and civilized lands, burning the towns and villages, killing the men,

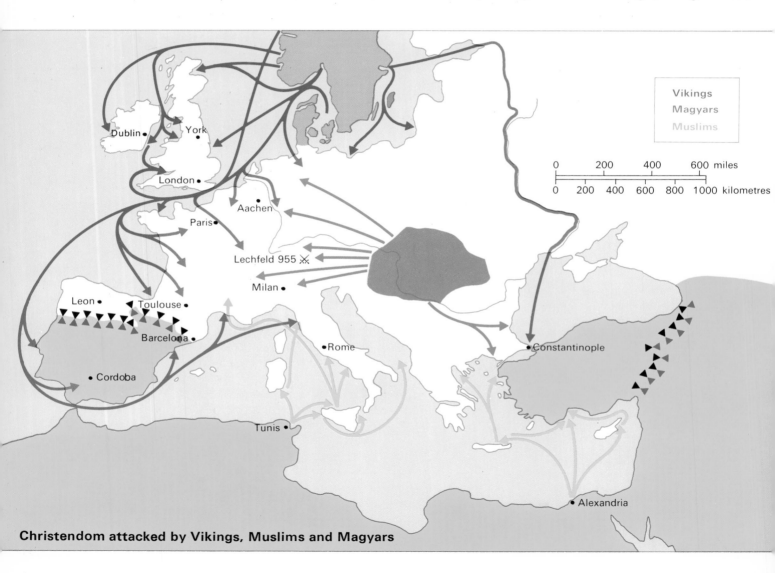

Christendom attacked by Vikings, Muslims and Magyars

A lord admits peasants to protection.

and driving away the women in gangs tied together by their long hair. To the dwellers of central Europe they were more dangerous than Vikings.

To make things worse still for the peoples of western Europe, Muslim pirates were still very busy in the Mediterranean, attacking the coasts of southern France and Italy.

For many years the kings of France and Germany seemed to be helpless. Sometimes their armies were beaten by the Vikings or Magyars. Sometimes they were too slow to catch them. Even when they did win a battle, the raiders soon recovered; they fled on their swift horses or warships, but they would be back, as dangerous as ever, next year or the year after. The people of France and Germany needed better protection than the king could give them.

The men who rose up in this time of trouble were the counts and dukes, the nobles who governed the marks and other districts. Each of them had his band of warriors, and each of them built a stronghold. Such a man could often defeat a small party of raiders, and if the raiders were too strong for a battle, the count could go with his people into his stronghold. Raiders were not looking for difficult sieges, if they could swerve away and pillage somewhere easier.

These local strong men could offer their people better protection than the distant king. But notice one thing. *Their* people. They demanded something in return. The peasants who wanted help had to pay in money, if they had it, or by giving food, or by working for the nobleman. They might have to offer even more, especially if the raiders had destroyed crops, herds and houses, and the peasants needed the count's help in starting life afresh. Often they had to agree never to leave their lord without his permission.

So the local noblemen became very powerful, each in his own district. They had to be, if anyone at all was going to survive the raids. They came to own most of the land in their districts, and practically own many of the people. This system was to go on long after the Magyars and Vikings had ceased to be a danger.

The Magyar menace was at last wiped out by the kings of Germany. The family of Charles the Great died out, so the most important nobles of Germany elected Duke Henry of Saxony to be their king. He had his plans. He made a truce with the Magyars, paying them tribute so that they would leave him

in peace. He used this peace to train his own men to fight on horseback as well as the Magyars could; and to build defences. Then, in 933, he stopped paying and was attacked once more by the Magyars. Henry's army gave them their first real defeat.

In 955 Henry's son Otto finished the job. Both sides brought all their strength to the battle of the Lechfeld. The Magyars broke, and for three days the Germans chased and killed them. They never came west again. About the year 1000 their king, St Stephen of Hungary, persuaded most of them to become Christians. Their savage nomad days were over.

The strong kings who had done this were more than ordinary kings. Both Henry and Otto took the title of Holy Roman Emperor. From this time onwards the Imperial Crown was worn only by the German kings (see the picture on the front cover). Other kings were willing to recognize the dignity of the title, especially when the emperor was a man like Otto. Gradually, though, the Holy Roman Empire came to be thought of as only the lands where the emperor really ruled; that is, Germany and northern Italy. There was no Lechfeld for the Vikings. Their victims had to wait for their 'fury' to die away.

The kingdom of England

Looking at what happened in England, we shall also be able to see the sort of thing that happened to the Northmen. Their raids changed to the attacks of armies and at last to national invasions. Britain was more exposed to Viking attacks than most places were, and it was in Britain that the Northmen met the only kings who were able to beat them.

The Great Army

By 865 the Danish Vikings had gathered together in a large army, had ravaged on the mainland of Europe, and decided on England as a suitable place for the next attack. Their judgment was sound. This map shows you what happened. One by one the Anglo-Saxon kingdoms either were defeated or gave in. The rival kings of Northumbria combined against the Danes, but were killed in battle after a fierce struggle. King Edmund of East Anglia was taken prisoner, refused to give up his Christian religion when the Vikings ordered him to worship their gods, and was shot to death with arrows; he is now known as St Edmund, and a town, Bury St Edmunds, is named after him. The king of Mercia, after a vain fight, fled to Rome.

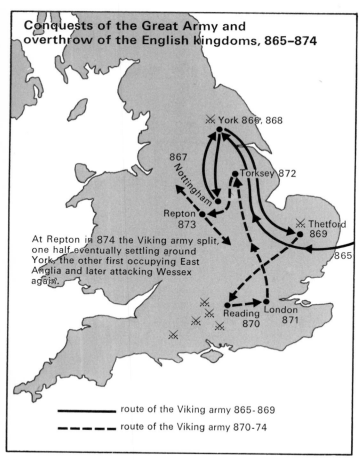

Conquests of the Great Army and overthrow of the English kingdoms, 865–874

York 866, 868

867

Nottingham

Torksey 872

Repton 873

Thetford 869

865

At Repton in 874 the Viking army split, one half eventually settling around York, the other first occupying East Anglia and later attacking Wessex again.

Reading 870

London 871

—— route of the Viking army 865-869
- - - route of the Viking army 870-74

Alfred's fight

Only the West Saxons were able to stand firm against the Great Army, and even they would have fallen if they had not been led by Alfred, the only English ruler who is known as 'the Great'. While a prince, he helped his elder brothers. When they died, and he was chosen king by the Witan, as the great council of bishops and nobles was called, he carried on with the struggle. He met the Danes in battle after battle. He did not win many victories, but he never gave in. At last the Danes grew tired of getting more hard knocks than loot, and agreed to accept a money payment and go away, in 871.

Six years later Alfred was treacherously attacked during the Christmas feast. Unable to fight, he fled to a secret refuge in the Somerset marshes, at a place called Athelney, and continued the fight. The tide turned. The West Saxons rallied. At the battle of Edington, in 878, the Danes were thoroughly beaten. They fled to their camp, and after Alfred had besieged them for two weeks, peace was made.

The Viking settlements

The Viking leader, Guthrum, and many of his chiefs (they were called jarls, and our modern title of earl comes from that word) were baptized Christians. They promised to go beyond Watling Street, and settle there, leaving Wessex and half Mercia free. This map shows you where they settled. You can also see where other Vikings were now settling in Britain, some Danish and others Norwegian. In those districts there are still many Viking place-names on the map. But Wessex was free. Alfred's next problem was: could he trust the Danes not to attack again? He decided to run no risks.

Alfred's defences

Guthrum was a man of his word, but there were other Vikings who had not sworn to the peace treaty. Wessex had to be ready. First, in case the country was caught by a surprise attack, Alfred ordered a large number of places to be fortified with ditch and rampart. These were called 'boroughs', and there were so many that most of the people would have a good chance of finding refuge in one. To try to catch any pirates before they had a chance to do harm, Alfred built warships. Also, he arranged that when he called for his people to come and join his army, only half at a time would come; the others would stay behind to look after the fields of the men with the army. By this, the king hoped that he would not be bothered by men trying to leave his army whenever they got anxious about the state of their crops.

This might hold back the Danes; in fact it did. But for the future Alfred wished to make his people better Christians, more educated and civilized. He saw that there was little point in winning his wars if his people at the same time lost their civilization; and the Danes had destroyed so many monasteries that there seemed to be a real danger of this. So, like Charles the Great, Alfred was a friend of learned men and a founder of monasteries. He went further. He himself translated and wrote books which he thought would educate his monks and nobles, if they would read them.

One king of all England

When he died in 899 Alfred left Wessex stronger than before the Viking attack. His son, Edward, and his grandson, Athelstan, renewed the war. This time it was the turn of the Danes to be attacked. By 954 it was all over. In that year Eric Bloodaxe, the last Viking king of York, was killed. The kings of Wessex were now kings of all England.

As it happened, England was to remain one kingdom from then onwards; though the kings were soon to change.

England as divided between Alfred and the Danes; and the Norse settlements in Britain, ninth to the eleventh centuries

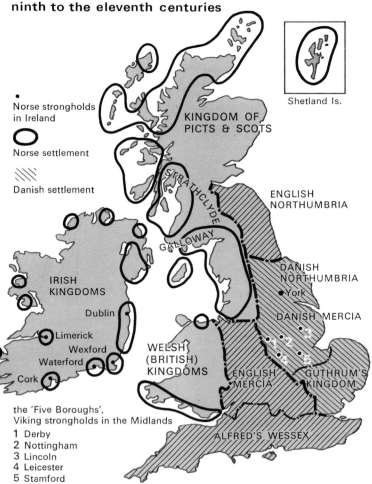

- • Norse strongholds in Ireland
- ⬭ Norse settlement
- ⧅ Danish settlement

Shetland Is.

KINGDOM OF PICTS & SCOTS

STRATHCLYDE

GALLOWAY

ENGLISH NORTHUMBRIA

DANISH NORTHUMBRIA
• York

IRISH KINGDOMS

Dublin

Limerick

Wexford

Waterford

Cork

WELSH (BRITISH) KINGDOMS

DANISH MERCIA

ENGLISH MERCIA

GUTHRUM'S KINGDOM

ALFRED'S WESSEX

the 'Five Boroughs', Viking strongholds in the Midlands
1 Derby
2 Nottingham
3 Lincoln
4 Leicester
5 Stamford

England, by comparison with other kingdoms of Europe in the tenth century, was well ruled. The king called his nobles and bishops to advise him; they formed his council, the Witan. In order to write and send out his letters and commands, to record his judgments and laws, the king had a very well trained group of clerks, a kind of small 'Civil Service' which was the best in Europe. To pay for an army there was a national tax, the Danegeld; no other European kingdom had such a thing. For local government and justice, the kingdom was divided into earldoms; these were divided into shires; and the shires were divided into areas called hundreds. If you look in your atlas you will notice how many English counties or shires take their name from the county town, especially in the Midlands. This is because where there was not already a convenient division, the shires were formed around boroughs.

New strength came into the church, too, and here also it came from the south-west. The three great leaders were St Dunstan, archbishop of Canterbury; St Oswald, bishop of Worcester and then archbishop of York; St Ethelwold, bishop of Winchester. They introduced from Europe a stricter version of the Rule of St Benedict to the English monasteries. New monasteries were founded by monks from the reformed older ones. From centres like Glastonbury and Abingdon and, a century later, Evesham new energy flowed. Great churches were built. Most of these have been destroyed, but enough remains of the smaller churches to give us an idea of what their builders and sculptors could do.

As peace and prosperity grew, English craftsmen, both inside monasteries and outside, produced rich and beautiful work as you can see from these pictures: jewellery of gold, precious stones and enamel; elaborately embroidered robes and hangings; fine carvings in wood and ivory; books in clear, rounded writing, with bright illuminations.

But all this does not mean that the people of England were one united nation. Some were Norwegians and Danes, living by their own customs; half of England was rightly called the Danelaw. Besides, men still thought of themselves as Mercians, or Northumbrians, or West Saxons rather than as Englishmen. As this map shows, the new earldoms into which the land was divided were very like the old kingdoms. What had been done to bring them together could easily be undone.

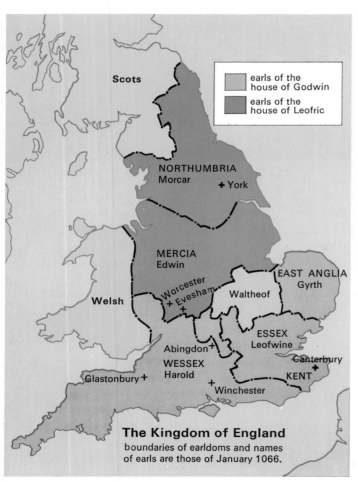

The Kingdom of England
boundaries of earldoms and names of earls are those of January 1066.

top right: Ivory carving of two angels, made at Winchester about 970. It is 3·05 in. (78 mm) high.

right: The Alfred jewel, probably made about 880. The lettering is *AELFRED MEC HEHT GEWYRGAN*, 'Alfred had me made'. The portrait in enamel may be of the king, or perhaps a saint whom Alfred particularly revered. The jewel is just under 2·5 in. (63·5 mm) long.

far right: In 966 King Edgar gave a foundation charter to the New Minster at Winchester. This is the title-page. It shows the king, standing between the Virgin Mary and St Peter, offering the charter to the King of Heaven.

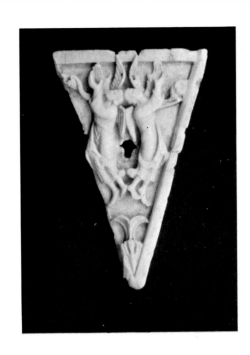

93

The Danes again

While the kings of Wessex were becoming kings of England, kings were also becoming more powerful in the home-lands of the Vikings. Sometimes this led to more peace in Norway, Sweden and Denmark, but sometimes it led to the king's enemies leaving his country and becoming Viking raiders. Sometimes the kings themselves became raiders. About a hundred years after the death of Alfred, Vikings attacked England again.

This time the king was very different from most of the English kings of those days. His name was Ethelred, which means 'Royal Counsel'; he won the nickname of Unred, which means 'No Counsel'. Everything he did went wrong.

He paid the Vikings to go away, using the money of the Danegeld. This need not have been a bad idea; as you saw on pages 66 and 89, the Byzantines and the Emperor Henry had done the same sort of thing. But they were strong, and Ethelred was weak; that was the difference, and that was why it did not work. When he tried to fight, he never succeeded.

So more and more Vikings came to collect money from the English king.

At last, desperate, Ethelred struck out. It was a terrible crime that he committed. Many Danes had taken his pay and promised to fight for him, and settled in and near London. London was a very important centre, as it had been in Roman times. Ethelred heard a rumour that they intended to rise against him. He panicked, and ordered his men to murder them all. This happened on St Brice's Day, 13 November, 1002. Among the dead was a sister of King Sven Forkbeard of Denmark.

The wars which followed did not end until 1017, when the English royal family were refugees in Normandy, and Sven's son Canute ruled as king of England.

Canute turned out to be a good king. He became a Christian; by now many of the Northmen were doing the same. He was king of Denmark already, and he conquered Norway. So there was peace at last round the North Sea.

His empire, though, did not last. Both of his sons became kings of England after Canute's death, and both died soon. In 1042 the English Witan offered the crown to the last of Ethelred's sons, Edward.

There was no fighting. Once again there was an English king in England. He was a good man, so religious that he is known as Edward the Confessor. But he was not tough enough for the job, and he had to allow his kingdom to be run by the strong Godwin, Earl of Wessex; and, after Godwin's death, by his son Harold. When Edward died in January, 1066, without children, it was no surprise that the Witan offered the crown to Harold Godwinson.

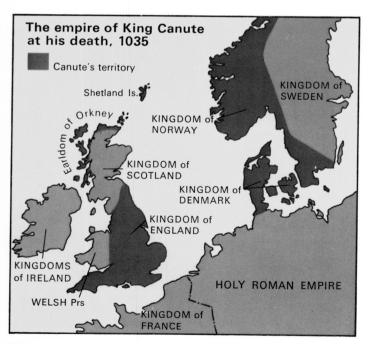

The empire of King Canute at his death, 1035

◼ Canute's territory

Shetland Is.
Earldom of Orkney
KINGDOM of NORWAY
KINGDOM of SWEDEN
KINGDOM of SCOTLAND
KINGDOM of DENMARK
KINGDOM of ENGLAND
KINGDOMS of IRELAND
WELSH Prs
HOLY ROMAN EMPIRE
KINGDOM of FRANCE

1066

The story of 1066 is one of the great tales of English history. It tells how Harold, the last English king, fought for the crown and all but won. It tells of the last successful invasion of England.

There were two other men who claimed that they should have the English crown. One was Harold Hardrada (which means 'The Hard Ruler'), who fought his way to the throne of Norway, and saw no reason why he should not be the heir to all the lands of Canute. The other was Duke William of Normandy, who from childhood had had to fight to defend his lands against the king of France, and who claimed that Edward had left the English crown to him, and that Harold Godwinson had promised to help him. This was probably true. Both of these men were mighty warriors, and the new king of England had to face both.

The answers to some very important questions depended on how the fight between the three rivals went:

Would the kingdom of England be linked again with the Viking lands?

Would England instead be linked with the south, the mainland of Europe?

Would England be able to stand alone, with no strong links either way?

Would the united kingdom of England fall apart under the strain, or be pulled apart by enemies?

Perhaps nobody at the time was able to put these questions quite as clearly as we can, for we have the enormous advantage of knowing the story from beginning to end. But whether the three rivals knew it or not – or even cared – they were going to decide the future, the very existence of the kingdom of England, in 1066.

Unfortunately for Harold Godwinson, both his enemies came against him at the same time. The map tells the story. While he was waiting for the attack of Duke William, who had been delayed all summer, partly by poor weather, Harold Godwinson heard that Harold of Norway, with a powerful Viking army, had landed near York. He marched his men north, and there was a great battle at Stamford Bridge. The Norsemen had come with 300 ships. The survivors needed only 24 to carry them back to Norway. Their king remained in England, dead.

While his battered army was resting after its hard-won victory, Harold Godwinson heard that William had come at last, and was laying waste Sussex. He had no choice. South he marched again, and gave battle on Senlac Hill.

When night fell on 14 October, of the three men who had claimed the throne of England, only William the Norman remained.

The campaigns of 1066: the triumph of Duke William the Norman

King Harold Hardrada's route

Stamford Bridge

York

King Harold Godwinson's route

ENGLAND

London

Hastings

Pevensey

Duke William's route

St Valery

English Channel

Somme

NORMANDY

vassal states of Normandy

BRITTANY   MAINE

friendly to William; allowed volunteers to help him

FRANCE

The Christian kingdoms of Europe

This book has been about the fall or decline of great empires. The Western Roman Empire broke up, and the attempt to revive it as the Holy Roman Empire was soon little more than a name for the German kingdom. The Eastern, or Byzantine, Empire was holding out, but had lost a lot of ground. The new Empire of the Caliph, though we have not had time to say much about it, had broken up.

Yet each of these Empires still lived on in men's minds, in the form of religion. Now almost all Europe was Christian. In the west, people followed the Pope; they were Roman Catholics. In the east, people looked for leadership to Constantinople, or Byzantium; these were Greek Orthodox. In the lands where the Arabs conquered, Islam prevailed. If you look at a modern map of the main religions, you will find that you can still recognize the picture.

In Europe, a new political pattern had appeared; again, it is one that you can recognize on the modern map. When the confusion of migrations, invasions and raids died away, most of the nations were settled where they live to this day; many of them were already ruled by their own kings. If you look at this map of Europe about 900 years ago, you will see modern Europe taking shape.

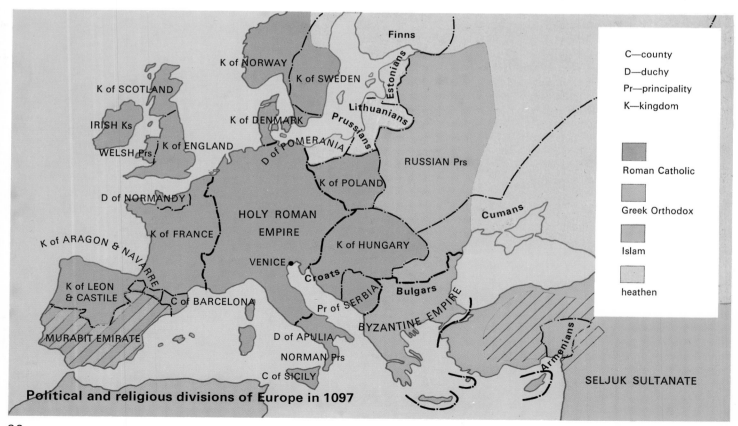

Political and religious divisions of Europe in 1097

Index

Adrianople, Turkey, 16
Africa, Byzantine influence in, 68
Aidan (bishop of Northumbria), 53
Alaric (king of the Goths), 16
Alcuin of York, 61, 82-83
Alexandria, Egypt, 68
Alfred the Great, 90-92
Angles, 23, 26-27
Anglo-Saxons: agriculture of, 32, 34-36; animal husbandry of, 36; churches of, 54; culture of, 11, 32-40; dwellings of, 32, 36-37; garments of, 38; gods of, 50; laws of, 39-40; money of, 39; oath helpers, 40; villages of, 35-37
Antioch, Turkey, 68
Arabia: culture of, 70; language of, 78; location of, 70-71; medical practice in, 79; scholarship in, 78-79
Arianism, 42
Arthur (king of Britain), 30
Athelstan (king of Wessex), 91
Attila, 18-19
Augustine (archbishop of Canterbury), 50-51
Aurelianius, Ambrosius, 30

Baghdad, Persia, 76
barbarian invaders of Britain: culture of, 8-9, 11; methods of conquest of, 26-28; settlement of, 26-27
barbarians of Europe: crafts of, 11; invasions into new territory of, 12-19; lands of, 13; laws of, 6, 10-11; livelihood of, 11; relics of, 7; settlement of, 20-21; social and political structure of, 6, 10-11, 17; warfare of, 11
basilicas, 41
Basilica Ulpia, Rome, 41
Bede, Saint, 51, 59

Bedouins, 72-73
Benedict, Saint, 44-45; Holy Rule of, 45, 55
Berbers, 74
bishops, authority of, 41
Boniface, Saint, 61
Book of Kells, 48
British coast, defense of, 24
Byzantine Empire. See Byzantium
Byzantium: Arab invasion of, 74; art of, 62-65; conflict with west of, 80-81; culture of, 62; defense of, 63, 66-69; in early Middle Ages, status of, 96; language of, 64; laws of, 64

Cadwallon (king of Wales), 52
Cairo, Egypt, 78
caliphs, 75-76
Canterbury, Archbishop of, 50
Canute (Danish king of England), 94
cathedrals, 41
Celtic monks. See monks, Irish
Charlemagne. See Charles the Great
Charles the Bald (king of France), 83
Charles the Great (Holy Roman Emperor), 61, 80-83
Christianity, Byzantine, 42-43, 62-63
Christianity, English, 46, 50-61
Christianity, European: English influence on, 61; rise of, 41-45
Christianity, Irish, 46-49, 55-57
Colman, Abbot, 56-57
Columba, Saint, 53
Constantine the Great (Roman emperor), 41
Constantine III (Roman-British emperor), 24
Constantinople. See Byzantium
Cordoba, Spain, 78

Damascus, Syria, 68
Danelaw, 92
Danes, conquests of, 94
Dunstan, Saint, 92

Eastern Empire. See Byzantium.
Ecclesiastical History of the English People, 51, 59
Ecgfrith (king of Northumbria), 58
Edmund, Saint, 90
Edward (king of Wessex), 91
Edward II (king of England), 94
Edwin (king of Northumbria), 52
Egypt, 74
England: beginnings of, 22; early arts and crafts of, 92; early organization of, 92; early scholarship in, 91-93; Viking traces in, 91
English language, Anglo-Saxon influence on, 28
Eric Bloodaxe (king of York), 91
Ethelbert (king of Kent), 50
Ethelred (king of England), 94
Ethelwold, Saint, 92
Ethiopia, 70, 74

feudalism, rise of, 89
forests, European, 6-13
Franks, 13, 16, 21, 75
Frisians, 13

Gaul (France), 16, 21
Germans, 21, 80, 96
Goths, 12, 16
Greek fire, 68-69
Greek Orthodox Church, 96
Gregory I, the Great (pope), 50-51
Guthrum, 91

Hagia Sophia (The Church of the Holy Wisdom), 63
Harold Godwinson (king of England), 94-95
Harold Hardrada, 95
Hastings, Battle of, 95
Henry of Saxony (king of Germany), 89
hermits, 42-43
Hijra. See Muhammed's Flight
Hilda, Saint, 53
Holy Roman Empire: decline of, 89, 96; division of, 83; early government of, 82-83; rise of, 80-83; scholarship in, 82-83
Hungarian barbarians. *See* Magyars
Huns: invasions of, 16; rise of, 14-15; social and political structure of, 14-15; warfare tactics of, 15, 18

Iona, 53, 57
Ireland, 22, 24
Islam: art of, 76-79; ascendance of, 72, 75; calendar of, 72; civilization of, 76-79; conquests of, 79; scholarship of, 78-79; spread of, 74-75

Jesus Christ, 42, 56
Justinian (emperor of Byzantium), 64-65
Jutes, 23, 26-27

king's hall, 38
Koran, 72

languages, European, 4-5
Leo I (pope), 18
life, price of. *See* wergild
Lindisfarne Gospels, 60
Lothar (Holy Roman Emperor), 83
Louis the German (king of Germany), 83
Louis the Pious (Holy Roman Emperor), 83

Magyar conquest, 88-89
Mecca, Saudi Arabia, 72
Mongolian hordes. *See* Huns
monks: Irish (Celtic), 55; Northumbrian, 55
Monte Cassino, 44-45
moot, 6, 10, 39-40
Mordred, 30
mosque, 76, 78-79
Muhammed, 70-74, 76
Muhammed's Flight, 70-71
Muslims. *See* Islam

Norman conquest, 95
Northumbria, England, 52-53, 56-59, 61
Nydam ship, 28

Offa (king of Mercia), 31
Ostrogoths, 12
Oswald, Saint (bishop of Worcester, archbishop of York), 92
Oswald, Saint (king of Northumbria), 53
Oswy (king of Northumbria), 56-58

Palestine, 74
patriarchs, 41
Patrick, Saint, 46
Persian Empire, 66, 68, 74
Peter, Saint, 56
Picts, 22, 24
popes, increase in political power of, 42

religious orders: English, 51-61; influence on culture of Europe of, 45-61; Irish, 46-50; rise of, 43-48
Roman Britain, fall of, 22-24
Roman Catholic Church, 42, 96
Roman Empire (Eastern). *See* Byzantium.
Roman Empire (Western): decline of, 17;

early Britain a part of, 24-25; fall of, 21; frontiers of, 12-13; invasion of, 16-17; language of, 4
Rome, Italy, 80
Roland, 80
Roncevalles, 80

Saint Brice's Day Massacre, 94
Saint Maria Maggiore, church of, Rome, 41
Saxons, 13, 16, 23, 26-27
Scots, 22, 24
slavery, 38, 40, 50, 72
Slavs, 21
Spain, 16
Stephen, Saint (king of Hungary), 89
steppes, Asian, 14-15
Stilicho (general of the Vandals), 16
Sueves, 16
Sutton Hoo ship, discovery of, 8-9, 28
Syria, 74

Theodore (archbishop of Canterbury), 57
Theodosius (emperor of Byzantium), 67
tonsure, 55

Vandals, 16
Verdun, treaty of, 83
Vikings: conquests of, 84-87; origins of, 84; raiding tactics of, 86-87; warships of, 84-85; weapons of, 86
Visigoths, 74
Vortigern (king of the Britons), 26

Wales, 4, 22-23, 31, 50
'Wanderer', 'The', 11
wergild (price of life), 10, 39
Wilfred, Saint, 56
William the Norman (king of England), 95
Witan, 92, 94

Acknowledgments

Illustrations in this volume are reproduced by kind permission of the following:
front cover, Kunsthistorisches Museum, Vienna; back cover, p.65, SCALA; pp.7 (Damendorf man), 28, Schleswig-Holsteinischer Landesmuseums, Schloss Gottorp, Germany; p.7, National Museum, Copenhagen; pp.8, 9, Colour Centre Slides Ltd; p.11, Det Denske Hedeselskabe, Viborg; pp.14, 21, Photographie Giraudon; p.24, Ministry of Public Buildings and Works; p.25, Scarborough Museum; pp.29, 30, 46, 57, 60, 83, 93, British Museum; pp.31, 34, 35, Dr J. K. St Joseph and the Cambridge University Department of Aerial Photography; p.37, after P. V. Addyman; p.38, Quentin Lloyd; pp.41, 45, Mansell Collection; p.42, Uppsala Universitetsbibliotek, Sweden; p.47, Irish Tourist Board; p.48, Board of Trinity College, Dublin; p.51, The Hermitage, Leningrad; pp.54, 57 (throne), 58, National Monuments Record; p.58, Edwin Smith (Ruthwell Cross); p.62, Museo Cristiana, Brescia, Italy; pp.63, 67, 78, 79, A. F. Kersting; p.64, Ecole Française d'Athènes; p.68, Alaric Toy; p.69, National Library Madrid and Archiv Mas; pp.72, 73, 76, J. E. Dayton; p.74, Edward de Unger, Esq.; pp.76 (dish), 77 (textile and crystal jug), Victoria and Albert Museum; p.77, York Minster (horn); p.78, J. Allan Cash (Cordoba mosque); p.79, Harold Ingram Esq. (Shrine); p.80, Réunion des Musées Nationaux; p.82, Dr Leo Hugot; p.85, Vikingeskibshallen, Roskilde, Denmark; p.86, London Museum; p.93, Winchester City Museums (ivory); Ashmolean Museum, Oxford (Alfred Jewel).

**Paintings and drawings by
Anne Mieke van Ogtrop
and Peter Whiteman
Maps by Peter Taylor
Diagrams by Banks and Miles**

front cover: The crown of the Holy Roman Empire. The main part was made for Otto the Great's coronation at Rome in 962.

The Cambridge History Library

The Cambridge Introduction to History
Written by Trevor Cairns

PEOPLE BECOME CIVILIZED   EUROPE AND THE WORLD

THE ROMANS AND THEIR EMPIRE   THE BIRTH OF MODERN EUROPE

BARBARIANS, CHRISTIANS, AND MUSLIMS   THE OLD REGIME AND THE REVOLUTION

THE MIDDLE AGES   POWER FOR THE PEOPLE

The Cambridge Topic Books
General Editor Trevor Cairns

THE AMERICAN WAR OF INDEPENDENCE
by R. E. Evans

LIFE IN THE IRON AGE
by Peter J. Reynolds

BENIN: AN AFRICAN KINGDOM AND CULTURE
by Kit Elliott

LIFE IN THE OLD STONE AGE
by Charles Higham

THE BUDDHA
by F. W. Rawding

MARTIN LUTHER
by Judith O'Neill

BUILDING THE MEDIEVAL CATHEDRALS
by Percy Watson

THE MURDER OF ARCHBISHOP THOMAS
by Tom Corfe

THE EARLIEST FARMERS AND THE FIRST CITIES
by Charles Higham

MUSLIM SPAIN
by Duncan Townson

THE FIRST SHIPS AROUND THE WORLD
by W. D. Brownlee

THE PYRAMIDS
by John Weeks

HERNAN CORTES: CONQUISTADOR IN MEXICO
by John Wilkes

THE ROMAN ARMY
by John Wilkes

LIFE IN A FIFTEENTH-CENTURY MONASTERY
by Anne Boyd

ST. PATRICK AND IRISH CHRISTIANITY
by Tom Corfe

The Cambridge History Library will be expanded in the future to include additional volumes. Lerner Publications Company is pleased to participate in making this excellent series of books available to a wide audience of readers.

Lerner Publications Company
241 First Avenue North, Minneapolis, Minnesota 55401